THE
MOMENT

William L. Fortune

progeny ✿ press
Villanova, Pa.

ISBN No. 0-934168-008.
Library of Congress Catalogue Card No.: 79-87489
Copyright© 1979 Progeny Press, Inc.
First Edition

With thanks to my wife, Jane, for her grace, understanding, and priceless aid in a sometimes graceless world, and the support of my loving children.

CONTENTS

v

Preface

"There is a tide in the affairs of men
which taken at the flood,
leads on to fortune
Omitted, all the voyage of their life
Is bound in shallows and in miseries."
                Julius Caesar, Act IV, Scene 3.

T HERE can be no doubt that there is a "tide in the affairs of men" and that such a critical "moment" can lead to personal success or failure. Without presuming too much, it can also be said that it may even affect the course of human history—sometimes its political course or at least the standards of achievement in the field in which that person attains success. It was a personal experience of this writer some years ago which first led him to this thesis—then to the readings of innumerable biographies and autobiographies to see if others had had similar experiences.

What was striking was that none of the biographers was particularly aware of the importance of this sometimes obscure moment (even when the biographee himself recognized it), or if he did take note, its importance was lost in the welter of other

facts that the biographer or writer was concerned
with. Could it be that the biographer himself lacked
the personal experience of such a "moment" or that
he failed to recognize it in his own life? For most of
us life has no historical significance. It's enough if
we recognize the critical importance of the person
we choose to marry, the school we attend or even
when we decide it is better to be honest than dishonest.

      Whether the person is historically impor-
tant or not, the essence of the "moment" is that it be
the critical juncture, the flood tide, from which all
future events in his life flow. There may be other
meaningful "moments"—and their relative importance can lead to endless speculation—but none
with the overwhelming significance to his personal
or perhaps history's future. We will be interested in
everything that led up to that "moment" and all that
flowed from it. None of the selections used were the
preconceived favorites of the author but rather
emerged as the most dramatic in the accounts which
are about to be related.

      In an age fraught with cynicism and pessi-
mism, it is hoped the reader will detect another
thread, besides the "moment", which pervades the
examples given. No matter at what age or what the
circumstances, each in his own way faced life with
hope, indeed, a bounding hope that said it would
overcome all obstacles in its path. One doesn't have

to be competing for the Presidency of the United States, or have the hidden talent of a best-selling writer, the physical grace of a Bobby Jones, the brain of a Lenin or the good instincts and wealth of a DuPont to weather the vicissitudes of life. Hope can be in the heart of a five year old girl, Sarah Bernhardt, or the will of a sixteen year old boy, Booker T. Washington. It can be in any of us, if we but will it.

A Personal Aside

"Aren't you a little young to be running for Treasurer of the State of Indiana?" the old timer asked the young (37) state legislator. Today he would think not, but in 1950 he would have to answer "yes." Then party discipline was strong and you waited your turn, especially when your opponent was a graying, elderly district chairman, party wheelhorse and friend of the powerful who were greatly in his debt for past favors.

"I know I am young, brash and headstrong, but that's what they said four years ago when I ran against the party slate and won a seat in the state legislature," I replied. "So why can't I do it again even though this is a far more difficult state-wide race?" "And I don't have much time."

"Don't have much time?" "What do you mean?"

"Well, there are many examples but one in particular stands out. As a boy, I was fascinated and inspired by Carl Sandburg's 'Lincoln', but there was one thing of particular interest. Do you realize in that one great life, devoted almost totally to politics and political

xi

activity from the age of 35 when he was first elected to
the Illinois Legislature until his assassination at 56, he
held only two important political positions? The first
turned out to be a dismal failure when as a Congressman
from 1847–1849 he cast one of the few votes against our
war with Mexico. For this he was considered a political
outcast—a pariah in his own party—and was denied reelection. The second, of course, was the Presidency in
1860 which lasted only four years and a few months into
his second term before he was assassinated. Thus, in a
life of thirty-five working years, he had served only a
little over six of those years holding political office.

"Now I may not be a Lincoln but wouldn't you
agree that the life of a politician is an extremely hazard-
ous and short-lived occupation—and that even at 37 my
time for serving in a public capacity may be very limited?"

The author had always been interested in politics. The genes must have been there from both grand-
fathers who served long and honorably in various civic
and public endeavors. But the match that kindled the fire
came from two great inspirational teachers of history at
Princeton University, "Buzzer" and "Beppo" Hall (not
related). Especially "Buzzer," so nicknamed for his deaf-
ness which disqualified him from normal duty in the
Spanish-American War but did not prevent him from
signing on as a cook for Teddy Roosevelt's Rough
Riders. "Buzzer's" patriotism was so intense that in-
variably when he gave his lecture on Garibaldi, the great

Italian freedom fighter, he would mount the top of his desk and pound it with his cane for greater emphasis to the delight of his standing-room only audience.

Thus inspired, the author went forth in the Great Depression years armed with a liberal arts degree and no discernible qualifications for business or a job. After six months of idle sloth at home, his family decided the only (and easy) answer was more education, and so he was shunted off to the Harvard Graduate School of Business where he idled away another year growing more and more weary of books and studying. It was especially dull for a restless young man who wanted to make his mark in the world of politics and/or journalism. Selling classified advertisements for Vogue Magazine could hardly be described as a journalistic endeavor, but it would have to do under the circumstances even if the pay was only $25.00 per week.

As every one knows Vogue is a woman's magazine catering to the fashionable shops of Fifth Avenue, New York. It wouldn't hurt, then, if her representative became somewhat fashion conscious. So he bought himself a derby and sprouted a dapper mustache to swagger his way through the elegant world of fashion hawking one and two-inch classifieds. "You are too reticent, too bashful to be a good salesman," a well-meaning possible client would tell him one day. The full truth of this came home to him when he realized he had not sold one advertisement in three months time. He knew then it was time

for him to admit to himself that this was not his métier
and really not even to his liking. So he made one telephone call to the west and then headed for the cornfields
of his native state. First, however, he got rid of the derby
and shaved his mustache knowing that Hoosiers frowned
on such signs of elegance.

Next he found himself reporting such worldly
events as the deliberations of The Daughters of Rebekah
(I.O.O.F.) and The Order of the Eastern Star for a daily
newspaper in northern Indiana. At least this was reporting (they called it cub reporting); this was journalism.
And soon it really was because on the next stop in Indianapolis, he landed a job with the respected, if poor,
now defunct Indianapolis Times, a Scripps-Howard
newspaper, first as City Hall reporter, then as State Political writer.

By November 1938 he felt secure enough to
marry a beautiful Irish girl with a delightful temperament and a rich sense of humor in a simple and brief
non-church wedding because of the groom's Protestant
background. Her good humor would be put to a test immediately as he whisked her away for a short week-end
honeymoon in Chicago climaxed by a romantic day-long
bus ride to a little town in northeastern Indiana.

There he had bought with $3,000 of the bank's
money a semi-weekly newspaper. Dunkirk was a town of
3,000 roustabout glass plant workers whose carousing
and fighting carried on through the night in the tavern

across the street from the newlyweds' apartment above the grocery store. The groom regretted exceedingly such an abbreviated wedding trip, but 1,000 subscribers were waiting breathlessly for the first issue of the new publisher's paper that Tuesday. It was not long before they were to feel somewhat cheated when the full-sized publication was transformed into a tabloid which would no longer fit their kitchen tables during the canning season.

But more important things were happening in the world beyond their small ken. The guns of war were rumbling throughout Europe. Within eight months of the United States' entrance in World War II, he was drafted as a private to serve his country. For the next three and one-half years he rose heroically through the ranks teaching venereal disease control and the hazards of malaria presented by the anopheles mosquito—until he was discharged a "buck" sergeant in late 1945. Now what was he to do? He had sold his newspaper and after that experience in independence he had no desire to work for someone else. He could always go back to school, especially now that it was being encouraged by veteran benefits. And a lawyer could be independent and still engage in political activities. So it was law school at night, studying and farming during the day (they had purchased a small farm on the outskirts of Indianapolis). But his restlessness knew no bounds. He was 35 years of age, well-educated, happily married with a small family and ambitious. Yet he often found himself staring blankly at

his law books wondering when, if ever, life would begin—when the "moment" came.

   Older and more experienced heads said it
couldn't be done. He would never be slated and nominated by his party for the state legislature without prior
service. First he must serve an apprenticeship as a precinct worker, taking the poll book, handing out literature, working at the polls on election day, helping other
candidates in their election efforts—all very menial tasks.
After several years of this, he might qualify himself for
election as precinct committeeman because then the party would owe something to him. But no, he was young
and he was headstrong and he would run for the Indiana
State Legislature anyway despite their advice. And, miracle of miracles, he would win both the nomination and
the fall election. He was on his way! The law was too
slow—it would have to wait. He would farm and "poli-
tic."

   Renominated for a second term in 1948, he
would lose in the fall election when the entire ticket went
down to defeat. But this would prove to be only a temporary set back. The 1949 session of the state legislature saw
to that when they made sweeping changes in the conduct
of the party conventions which nominated the Governor,
Lt. Governor, U.S. Senator, Treasurer of State and other state officials. Probably the most significant change
was the institution of voting machines to record the votes
of the delegates secretly. Prior to that time all power rest-

ed in the hands of the party county chairman who voted his county delegation just about any way he pleased. He, in turn, worked closely with his district chairman, and the eleven district chairmen worked hand-in-hand with the state chairman. Thus, the power structure resembled a pyramid with the state chairman at the top brokering down through the district chairmen who worked with the county chairmen to determine the party's nominees for state office. If the delegates didn't conform or cooperate, they would not be returned as delegates to the next convention.

Now the power, for the first time in Indiana history, was suddenly transferred to the delegates who voted as they wished in secret ballot. The power brokers were slow to recognize the magnitude of this change. But the candidate and his friends sensed it and sought to capitalize on it. All that spring and early summer of 1950 he travelled thousands of miles throughout the state in his quest for the nomination for Treasurer of State, visiting individually and on a person-to-person basis all the county chairmen and over half of the 2,000 delegates who were likely to attend the state convention. He talked to them in the fields on their tractors, in their homes and stores, at plant gates and on street corners—wherever he could find them—even in a coal mine. His opposition was a long-time district chairman and party wheelhorse who stayed at home and relied on his friendship and the backing of the state chairman to deliver the nomination to him.

The result was a totally unexpected two to one victory for the young (37) political neophyte on the first ballot. The office hardly warranted the attention, but the next morning the Indianapolis Star gave recognition to its unusual nature when they banner headlined the story on the front page with "FORTUNE WINS TREASURER NOMINATION." "That's pretty heady stuff," the Indiana manager of Associated Press would warn him. And it was. His election that fall was an anticlimax. But he could always take pride in the thought that his nomination, although it was but a fly speck on the historical process, had forever changed the method of campaigning for state political office in Indiana. Two years later it was a different story. The political bosses had learned their lesson only too well and the new Treasurer of State failed to recognize it.

Within six months as Treasurer he had surveyed the method by which former Treasurers had deposited the state's surplus funds and found that they had overwhelmingly favored the large city banks over the small country banks of which there were roughly 400 in the state. There was no statute against this practice. It was just patently unfair. So he devised a formula whereby every bank in the state would share in the state's largess equally on the basis of their capital and existing deposits. This meant a complete reversal of the state's policy and a reallocation of about one-quarter of the state's funds from the city banks to the country banks. The president of one of Indiana's largest banks, when he heard the story, rushed over to one of the newspapers and begged them not to print the story because "there was nothing unusual about it." The newspaper was not impressed; they printed it anyway, as their lead story on the front page that day.

Although it was not calculated as such, this one move immediately catapulted the Treasurer into the forefront of the race for the nomination for Lt. Governor in the 1952 convention. He campaigned just as hard and thoroughly as he had for the Treasurer's nomination, thinking that if anything his popularity had been enhanced by his record of fairness as Treasurer. It had. But he naively assumed that this alone would carry the day as it had before. He did not realize that this time the political bosses, led by the dominant political power in the state, U.S. Senator William E. Jenner, and his state chairman, were playing "hard ball." Their candidate was a Jenner crony, a personable but colorless state senator without any particular record to commend him. More importantly, they had persuaded three or four other candidates to enter the fray, each with his own following and each willing to throw their support to the state senator if their own race faltered. Little things count. The leading candidate and his attractive family were assigned to an upper tier box somewhat hidden by those in front and isolated from friends and delegates on the floor below.

The first ballot told the story. The leading candidate didn't lead. He fell behind by only 30 votes (out of

2,000), but that was enough to make it fatal. On the second ballot, it was all over as each of the other candidates withdrew from the race and asked their supporters to cast their votes for the opposition. As the Treasurer and his family left the convention hall, passing delegates found reason to look aside or downward, and there were few good-byes. Hours later the candidate and his family were still staring at the open spaces on their farm, too stunned or maybe too hurt to say anything to each other about it. The moment and the momentum were gone, never to return again.

I

LADY LUCK

THOMAS WOODROW WILSON
"We thought it was all over"

A. J. CRONIN
"The floodtide of success was loosed."

Thomas Woodrow Wilson

"Human life is more governed by fortune than by reason."
David Hume, Scottish Philosopher (1711–1776)

Fate, chance, or, if you will, the wheel of fortune, played the greatest role in the nomination and therefore, election of the 28th President of the United States—a Presidency which would involve the United States in its first world-wide conflict and its eventual emergence as a world power. The central figure in the Democratic National Convention of 1912 was not its nominee, Thomas Woodrow Wilson, the Governor of New Jersey, who was resting passively at his summer cottage in Sea Girt, N.J., one hundred miles away from the convention site; it was his floor managers.

"I have no deep stakes involved in this game," he would tell his intimates on the eve of the convention as the delegates gathered together in the 5th Regiment Armory in Baltimore, Maryland, on a hot, steamy Tuesday, June 25. "I have not the least idea of being nominated because the make-up of the convention is such, the balance of forces, that the outcome is in the hands of the professional politicians who serve only their own interests and who know that I will not serve them except as I might serve the party in general." The scholarly ex-President of Princeton University had every reason to be dejected—the conservatives were clearly in control of the convention machinery having nominated Judge Alton B. Parker of New York as temporary chairman over William J. Bryan, the perennial choice of the progressives for anything, who was also supported by Wilson. And in all the pre-convention primaries between January and April, the other leading candidate, Champ Clark, Speaker of the House of Representatives—safe, conservative, dependable and colorless—had swept everything before him. Even Bryan's home state of Nebraska went for Clark. And Wilson's birthplace, Virginia, not wishing to back a loser or insult their native son, chose to send an uninstructed delegation to the convention.

The meteoric rise of the former college President to the Governorship of New Jersey appeared to be at an end despite his outstanding record. Until now he had played the political game with a finesse and skill belying his scholarly background. It had all begun only two years before in January of 1910 when Wilson's friend, Colonel George Harvey, editor of Harper's Weekly and a person with many influential conservative friends, had sat down for lunch at that famous meeting place for politicians, Delmonico's, with the political boss of New Jersey, ex-U.S. Senator James Smith, Jr.

Harvey's mission on that cold, wintry day was

to try and persuade the "boss" to accept Wilson as the Democratic party's gubernatorial nominee at the state convention in September. At first, Smith was wary of the "Presbyterian Priest," as he would call him, fearful that he would not be a party "regular" and play the political game as Smith and his organization wanted it. As usual, Smith's political instincts were unerring, but he also knew that a party boss must win elections in order to stay in power. And he did not have to be reminded that the Democrats had been consistent losers since the Civil War or that they had won only two national elections since then (both under Grover Cleveland in 1884 and 1892). It was dusk before the two weary men stepped out onto Williams Street, but Smith had capitulated and promised Col. Harvey he would back Wilson for the nomination if Wilson would accept it.

In the meantime, Wilson's career at Princeton had reached a critical point in his constant struggle with alumni and trustees over his progressive educational ideas. In April, he confided to a friend that his life had been a failure as he publically criticized alumni groups in New York and Pittsburgh for "siding with dollars rather than ideas." Still he would play the role of the reluctant candidate when Col. Harvey told him that the gubernatorial nomination could be handed to him on a "silver platter." "I will give the matter serious consideration," is all that Wilson would say to him.

Then, on Sunday, April 26, 1910 Col. Harvey, "Boss" Smith and Col. Henry Watterson, the noted edi-

tor of the Louisville Courier-Journal, met at Deal, New
Jersey, and formally pledged their support to Wilson for
the nomination to be held at the Democratic State Convention in Trenton, New Jersey, on September 15.
Now, virtually assured of the nomination, Wilson finally
on July 15 wrote the newspapers and said he would consider it his duty to accept if "a majority of the thoughtful
Democrats of the state wanted him to." The vote of the
convention was closer than any one had anticipated, but
the machine of "Boss" Smith finally carried the day for
Wilson. But he had won by less than 100 votes out of
over 1,400 that were cast. Had it not been for the eloquence and sincerity of the nominee's acceptance speech,
which served to heal the party's wounds, Wilson might
never have gone on to victory in the November election.

One could speculate that it was Wilson's ambition to seek a political career through the Governorship
of a major state or that his desire to carve out a new career for himself was motivated by frustration in accom-
plishing his educational goals. The truth would always
be locked behind that characteristic reserve for which he
was so well known. The fact remains, however, that
once he had embarked on his new career he brought to it
all the determination, obstinacy and shrewd instincts of
one who had been born to it—and one additional factor
not usually found in politicans, a stoical sense bordering
on fatalism.

But his most immediate problem came in the
form of an announcement by former Senator James

Smith, the political boss, that he would again seek election to the U.S. Senate when the legislature met in January. In the early 1900's it was the state legislatures which elected the U.S. Senators, not the people as it is today. Wilson would not take office until mid-January, but he knew now that whatever legislative program he would propose would be ground to mincemeat by the Smith machine if Smith won reelection and continued to dominate the Democratic party in New Jersey. Wilson had no choice but to fight the reelection of his former mentor.

Smith knew this too and accepted the challenge on a winner-take-all basis for the political supremacy of the state. It came in the form of an ultimatum from Wilson that Smith either withdraw from the race in 48 hours or face an open state-wide fight before the bar of public opinion. Smith chose to fight. And so on December 9, only five weeks before the legislature was to convene, Wilson publically proclaimed his support for a political nonentity, one James Martine and forthwith set out on a feverish campaign of mass meetings to marshall public support for his man. He was very much alone, fighting a powerful, entrenched political machine without money or an organization to back him up. "If he had failed," his biographer, Ray Stannard Baker, would write later, "he could not have secured the reform measures he desired from the legislature and he could not have challenged in the national field Roosevelt's or LaFollette's or Bryan's power as the spokesman for liberalism." And he did not

fail. The Wilson forces demolished the Smith machine 5
to 1 when the legislature met. It was a critical juncture in
the life of Woodrow Wilson.

Within two years an even greater drama was to
be fought out by a far less persistent and more fatalistic
candidate for the Presidency of the United States in the
longest (up to that time) national convention in the history of the United States. Wilson's principal antagonist
and rival in the drama for the Presidency was the Speaker of the House of Representatives, Champ Clark, a representative of the conservative wing of the party and, by
all odds, the front runner. But by the rules of the game at
that time, he had to muster two-thirds of the 1,000 voting delegates before he could claim the nomination. But
the nomination would almost be tantamount to election
since the Republicans were hopelessly split between the
conservative forces of the incumbent President, William
Howard Taft, running for reelection, and the progressives led by Theodore Roosevelt who had bolted the regular party convention.

Wilson's principal supporters were: his floor
manager, William F. McCombs, a New York lawyer and
former student of Wilson's at Princeton, probably the
first man to actively support Wilson, a cripple and a
"neurotic whose ambitions far exceeded his capacity"
and another New York lawyer, William G. McAdoo, six
feet tall, "wiry, sinewy, tireless with a hawk-like face and
a southern burr . . . fertile in all resources of organiza-

tion," urbane and imperturbable. He was best known for his struggles with the New York financial interests over the development of the tunnels under the Hudson River. Later he would become Wilson's Secretary of the Treasury and the first Chairman of the Federal Reserve Board. Finally, there was that firebrand of oratory, thrice his party's nominee for the Presidency, the next Secretary of the State, William Jennings Bryan, fearless leader of the progressive forces of the West against the conservative East led by Tammany Boss Thomas E. Murphy, and financiers J. P. Morgan, August Belmont of New York and Thomas Fortune Ryan of Virginia.

Meanwhile, Wilson, his family and Joseph P. Tumulty, his confidant and private secretary who was an attorney and had been a member of the New Jersey General Assembly, had taken up residence at the Governor's summer cottage in Sea Girt, New Jersey for the duration of the convention. They maintained constant contact with their headquarters in the Emerson Hotel in Baltimore through the wire services and a private telephone line.

As we have seen, all the events leading up to the convention, including the state primaries and state conventions and now the election of a temporary chairman for the convention had been dominated by the conservative forces within the party and their candidate, Champ Clark. In fact, their control was so great that a little over a month before the convention, Wilson would write a friend ". . . when I see vast sums of money poured out against me, with fatal success . . . it begins to look as if I must merely sit on the sidelines and talk, as a mere critic of the game I understand so intimately." And then again on May 26, 1912 he would write to another friend: "the world . . . so brutal, so naked of beauty, so devoid of chivalrous sentiment and all sense of fair play that one's spirit hardens. . . . I fight on in the spirit of Kipling's IF ('and so hold on when there is nothing in you except the Will which says to Hold on!')." "But that is oftentimes a very arid air," he added with a touch of whimsy.

And so it was that a thoroughly embittered and discouraged Wilson took up his listening post at Sea Girt, knowing that his campaign organization was torn asunder with internal difficulties, that it was nearly bankrupt and that even his national headquarters in New York city was virtually deserted. And now the opposition had put one more nail in his coffin by electing the temporary chairman of the convention. By tradition the temporary chairman almost always became the permanent chairman and it was his prerogative to recognize or just ignore any requests coming from the Wilson people on the floor. Wilson had allied himself with the progressive forces when he wrote Bryan "The Baltimore convention is to be a convention of progressives . . . and must express (this) in its choice of men who are to speak for it."

But just as everything looked the darkest, Tumulty received word at Sea Girt that Judge Parker had not been elected as permanent chairman. Instead the post had gone to Congressman Ollie M. James of Kentucky, a friend of Bryan's. Bryan had so dramaticized the fight over the chairmanship and the battle between the liberal and conservative forces that 110,000 telegrams poured into the convention halls, thus tipping the scales in favor of Bryan's man. Wilson would never have been nominated, had Bryan had an unfriendly chairman, the dean of the political columnists at that time, Frank R. Kent, wrote in the Baltimore Sun. In fact, Bryan's effort to place an explosive resolution before the convention in its third day, even before any names had been placed in nomination, would not have been recognized, had there been an antagonistic chairman. The resolution would put the convention on record as being opposed to any candidate "under obligation to J. Pierpont Morgan, Thomas F. Ryan, August Belmont or any other member of the privilege-hunting, favor-seeking class." The resolution carried by an overwhelming 4 to 1 margin. Even the conservatives found it difficult to vote against such high standards of public probity.

Already the convention was three days old, almost as long as a modern day political convention lasts in total, and not one name, the primary purpose of the convention, had been placed in nomination for the Presidency of the United States. By midnight Thursday, however, all the preliminary activity, jockeying for position and resolution-making had taken place, and the delegates settled back to listen to the endless nominating and seconding speeches.

By breakfast Friday morning all the names of the expected candidates had been placed in nomination— Speaker of the House Champ Clark, Governor Wilson and a favorite of Wilson's, even though he was a conservative, the able and courageous chairman of the House Ways and Means Committee, Oscar W. Underwood of Alabama, who was considered an authority on tariffs. A fourth and unexpected name was added, the able but dull Governor of Ohio, Judson Harmon, representing the extreme right wing of the party. However, his candidacy was not expected to get anywhere, its only purpose being to hold New York's large block of 90 votes until such time as Boss Murphy would decide to throw them to his favorite, Clark, in the hope of starting a stampede.

The first ballot was taken at 7 a.m. that morning, with predictable results. The weary, sleepless delegates cast 440½ votes for Clark, 324 for Wilson, 148 (including all of New York's 90) for Harmon and 117½ for Underwood. No candidate had a majority of the votes cast much less the two-thirds necessary for nomination. Balloting continued relentlessly throughout the day with little change. As they approached the ninth ballot, McAdoo, who was a member of the New York delega-

tion, received word from a friend in the delegation who
was also close to Tammany Hall that Boss Murphy
planned to throw all their chips in on the 10th ballot in an
effort to stampede the convention for Clark. The vote
would come late that night or early Saturday morning.

McCombs, Wilson's floor manager, froze in his
tracks when he heard this news. No one could be nominated without New York's votes and he was obsessed in
his efforts to get these votes. He also knew, as every other delegate in the 5th Regiment Armory knew, that this
would mean a narrow majority for Clark and no candidate in the 68 years of convention history had failed to
go on and receive the necessary two-thirds once he had
breached that point.

But there were others in the Wilson camp—
particularly McAdoo, A. Mitchell Palmer of Pennsylvania (later Wilson's Attorney General) and the ram-
bunctious W. H. ("Alfalfa Bill") Murray of Oklahoma
(later Governor)—who refused to be daunted. It was
their decision, which prevailed, to treat the whole thing
as matter-of-factly as possible despite its obvious importance and the tremendous floor demonstration which
took place after it was announced. McAdoo was everywhere on the convention floor pleading and urging delegates to stand firm. Fortunately, some strong Wilson
states followed New York on the roll call, but none were
more pivotal in stemming the tide than Oklahoma and
the bull voice of "Alfalfa Bill" Murray. When a Clark
delegate asked that the Oklahoma delegation be polled,

"Alfalfa Bill", who as usual was coatless and had his red bandana handkerchief tied around his neck, rose from his chair, snapped his famous "galluses" and in that booming stentorian voice of his which could be heard to the far reaches of the hall roared that he had no objection to the polling, but ". . . we do insist we shall not join Tammany in making the nomination!"

At 1 a.m. Saturday the vote was tallied and Wilson had lost only two votes from the previous ballot. Clark had his majority with 556, Wilson had 350½, Underwood 117½ and Harmon 31. Wilson lines had obviously held, but the pressing question now was could they withstand any further onslaughts and if they did, how could they overcome the seemingly insurmountable 200 vote margin now favoring Clark, the bandwagon psychology and the impatience of bone-weary delegates wanting to get it over with and go home. There was one very important person, Wilson's floor manager, who didn't think he could. And McCombs thought it was his duty to tell him so.

Early Saturday morning Wilson received a telephone call from McCombs. Mrs. Wilson and Tumulty were in the room at the time and overheard Wilson's end of the conversation:

"So, McCombs, you feel it is hopeless to make further endeavors," they heard him say. "No, I cannot ask my friends to support Underwood or any other candidate, but please tell them how greatly I appreciate their generous support and they are now free to support any candidate they choose." With this, he hung up the receiver. Mrs. Wilson, in tears, went over to him, tenderly put her arms around his neck and said "My dear Woodrow, I am sorry, indeed, that you have failed." Wilson smiled and with little evidence of disappointment looked down on her and said "My dear, of course I am disappointed, but we must not complain. We must be sportsmen. After all, it is God's Will and I feel a great load has been lifted from my shoulders. Now we can take that long awaited vacation to Rydal (the English lake country)." Then, turning to Tumulty, he asked for a pencil and pad saying "I will prepare a message of congratulations to Champ Clark. He will be nominated and I will give you a message in a few minutes." Thus Wilson appeared to reconcile himself to defeat.

At 10 a.m. that same morning in Baltimore, after only four hours sleep, McAdoo entered McCombs' hotel room. McCombs was in an hysterical state.

"The jig is up," McCombs said. "Clark will be nominated."

"Do you mean you are giving up the fight?" McAdoo asked.

"Why, Governor Wilson himself has given up," McCombs replied, "and I will receive a telegram to this effect any time now."*

"You have betrayed the Governor and you have sold him out," McAdoo shouted as he rushed to the telephone to put in a call to Governor Wilson.

"Governor, I have just talked to McCombs who

is in the room with me about your conversation with him. I am duty bound to tell you that the information he gave you is completely erroneous; in fact, you are gaining strength all the time and Clark will never receive the necessary two-thirds vote. I plead with you not to release your delegates and not to give up the fight."

"My dear McAdoo, this is very difficult for me to believe, but I did instruct McCombs not to release any delegates without conferring with you and getting your approval."

"Then, do I have your permission to countermand any previous instruction you have given McCombs?" he asked.

"Yes you have," Wilson replied, "but let me talk to McCombs." Whereupon Wilson got on the phone with McCombs and confirmed everything he had said to McAdoo.

And so it is that sometimes the great events of personal and world history turn on the fragile, ephemeral quicksands of time. "Looking back, one is impressed by the hair-trigger chances of that unprecedented convention!" Mr. Wilson's biographer, Ray Stannard Baker, observed. "A single misstep and Wilson would have lost."

Only three hours separated these telephone conversations and the reassembly of delegates at convention hall at 1 p.m. Did Wilson mean to concede defeat? It would appear so. We will never know if such a wire conceding defeat was ever sent, because there is none in his private papers, but we do have Mrs. Wilson's word that "we thought it was all over," and that such a wire was in fact sent to McCombs. The fact remains had not McAdoo made his fortuituous visit to McCombs' room that morning, McCombs would have had ample time to have spread the news of Wilson's concession. The effect on Wilson's candidacy would have been devastating and irreversible and, as McAdoo would observe in his autobiography years later, "the history of the next ten years would have presented a different picture of the world."

All day Saturday the balloting continued. Although Wilson reached his nadir on the 10th ballot, his progress was so glacier-like (three or four votes gain on each ballot) that neither he nor his friends could relax or afford the slightest misstep. "At the present rate of gain I will be nominated in 175 more ballots," Wilson commented wryly. Even Bryan's dramatic announcement from the convention floor on the 14th ballot that he would never support a candidate who had the backing of the New York delegation or any one not free to uphold the convention's anti-Morgan-Ryan-Belmont resolution produced no measurable upsurge in Wilson's strength. By the end of the day on the 26th ballot, the vote still favored Clark with 463$\frac{1}{2}$ votes to Wilson's 407$\frac{1}{2}$.

But Wilson could relax a little now since his lines were holding and it was Saturday and the convention would be recessed over the Sabbath. He might well have mused that the fates had been kind to him when McAdoo interceded with McCombs to save his candidacy from certain defeat. And being a student of history, he would know that it was not always this way. For instance, he would remember that another politician, centuries ago and in a different political climate, would plan and plot his career, leaving as little as possible to chance. Julius Caesar would take the supreme gamble of his career at an early age, but it would be a calculated one, one that was planned and one that if he won it, would give him a power base for future political successes. Losing, he might have lost all, but this history will never know.

For now the future President could think back and realize that he had had more control over his destiny as Governor of New Jersey than he did now running for the Presidency. Even though the Governorship had been handed to him "on a silver platter", he made the critical decision to fight for his reforms in the legislature against the powerful Smith political machine. And in doing so unwittingly he became a figure of national prominence— someone others would talk about as being a possible Presidential candidate someday. Another Governor of the time—John A. Dix of New York—chose another course saying such matters were for the state legislature to solve—and he passed into oblivion.

He would also wonder if such critical moments happened only to the ambitious and talented people and he would conclude that these were the cases that every one would read or hear about. But, philosopher that he was, he knew that they must happen also in the life of very ordinary people although the occasion might not be so dramatic nor as well-known. For instance, he thought, it might be in the person we marry or the moment we decide very simply that it is better to be honest than dishonest. This happens to all of us, but sometimes we are not even conscious of it until after it has happened. Then we look back and say to ourselves, yes, I didn't know it, but that was the precise moment, all-determining in nature, from which everything else in my life flowed.

It was a beautiful day as Mr. and Mrs. Wilson traveled to Spring Lake, New Jersey, to attend church. After the services Reverend Dr. James M. Ludlow expressed surprise to them that they had traveled such a distance to attend church. "Why, doctor, where should a man in my straits be on such a day, except in the House of God," Wilson replied.

Meanwhile, in Baltimore, the Sabbath received little respect from the political jackals who continued the maneuvering and conniving to whittle away at Wilson's strength. In an effort to win over the Pennsylvania delegation, the Clark people offered the vice-presidential nomination to one of Wilson's staunchest supporters, the leader of that delegation, A. Mitchell Palmer, later to become Wilson's Attorney General, but Palmer would not be enticed. And even within his own camp, McCombs continued to persist in his efforts to get Wilson to take an anti-Bryan position by asking Wilson to promise that he would not name Bryan his Secretary of State. He refused. So if Wilson seemed to falter, almost fatally, to his floor manager's inducements to withdraw from the contest after the 10th ballot, it is to his great credit that on two other occasions—the Bryan anti-Morgan-Ryan-Belmont resolution at the beginning of the convention which he supported against McCombs' advice and now the effort to deny Bryan a possible cabinet position, he stood steadfast, much to his advantage.

On Monday, July 1, two significant events took place. The country's leading Democratic newspaper, the New York World, declared itself in favor of Wilson with a resounding editorial by Frank I. Cobb. Now Wilson had the support of all 27 Scripps papers, of which the World was the flagship paper, and also the Baltimore Sun and the august New York Times. Next on the opening ballot of the day (the 27th) the first large state delegation, Indiana, under the leadership of Senator Tom Taggart, broke away and cast 29 of its 30 votes for Wilson. Up to now Indiana had supported its favorite son, Governor Thomas R. Marshall who later became Wilson's running mate as the vice-presidential nominee. "From that time on Clark's strength disintegrated with every ballot," McAdoo would write in his autobiography. Three ballots later (the 30th) Wilson passed Clark for the first time—460 to 455—and by the end of the day on the 42d ballot the vote stood 490 for Wilson and 430 for Clark, which was still considerably short of the necessary two-thirds for nomination. The dike had been breached and events would move inexorably to a swift conclusion.

The following morning, Tuesday, July 2, the convention (now a week old) opened with the usual prayer, but there was a sense of anticipation and excitement in the air that this was not going to be just another day of long, tedious balloting and stalemate. It was going to be different. Rumors were rife but mostly centered on speculation as to which state, especially among the larger ones, was going to be the one that would tear open the already ruptured dike to let the torrent of Wilson votes through from the flood plain behind. The clerk started to call the roll of states for the first ballot of the day. The voting, as it came in alphabetical order, remained just about as it had on the previous day—until it reached Illinois. "Illinois, how do you vote?" the clerk asked. Slowly the head of the delegation rose from his chair as thunderclaps of shouting and cheering started to roll through the hall in anticipation of what was coming. "Mr. Chairman, Mr. Chairman," he shouted to raise his voice above the bedlam of noise. . . ."Mr. Chairman, I, Roger Sullivan, chairman of the delegation from the great state of Illinois, home of another great American, Abraham Lincoln, cast all 58 of its votes for the next President of the United States, Thomas Woodrow Wilson." And the stampede was on. Three ballots later (the 46th), the longest political convention in the history of the United State up to that time came to an end—after eight days. At 3:30 p.m. Wilson with 990 votes went over the top and was declared the Democratic party's official nominee for the Presidency of the United States in the 1912 election.

Wilson received word of his nomination in his study at Sea Girt while his wife was resting in her upstairs bedroom. He wanted to be the first to tell her. Quietly he walked up the stairs so as not to disturb her if she were asleep, opened the door and finding her awake, went over to her as if to kiss her. Then stopping at her bedside, he smiled and said "Well, dear, we won't go to Rydal after all." And then he kissed her.

Wilson would soon realize that because of the serious split in the Republican party between the conservatives under William Howard Taft and the progressives under Teddy Roosevelt, his nomination virtually assured him of the election to the Presidency. Edward Gibbon once said, "The winds and waves are always on the side of the ablest navigators." And so it may have been with Wilson. Except for his fatalistic attitude ("it's God's Will") and near acceptance of defeat on the 10th ballot, wherein he was saved from himself by the pure luck of circumstance and the strong will of McAdoo, Wilson's elemental political shrewdness and astute assessment of the larger events leading to his nomination were faultless.

His insight into the opposing forces in the convention and his handling of them may have been far more skillful than any one at the time realized. There can be no doubt about the honesty of his liberal leanings, as indicated by his record as Governor and President. Yet it cannot be overlooked that politically he was capable of and did play both sides of the street with considerable skill. He was the all too willing hand-picked nominee of the conservative New Jersey bosses (against whom he turned once elected). And knowingly, if not designedly, he balanced the efforts of McCombs to win over the conservatives at the national convention (McCombs was never repudiated) with, as Tumulty would relate, a calculated drive through McAdoo and others to win the support of Bryan and the progressives.

If the 10th ballot was the essence of the critical moment including the circumstances surrounding his near capitulation and sure failure, almost as remarkable was the tenuous balance that had to be maintained for three more days and sixteen more ballots in the sweltering July heat of a convention hall which then had no air-conditioning. Had the Clark forces at any time during this critical period of strained tempers made any substantial inroads into the Wilson strength like the New York conversion, there is no doubt, as McAdoo later said, the momentum would have shifted to Clark and history would have told a different story in Baltimore that week and for years to come.

* There is no record in Wilson's papers of such a telegram, but on July 2 a reporter for the Baltimore Sun quoted Mrs. Wilson as saying: "There was a time when we felt dubious about this and despaired of success. Things looked so dark when Mr. Clark received a majority that Mr. Wilson sent a message to Mr. McCombs releasing the Wilson delegates . . . Mr. Wilson thought that it was all over, and we tried to pretend to think we were glad that it was over." (Woodrow Wilson's Life & Letters—Vol. III—by Ray Stannard Baker, Page 352)

A. J. Cronin

"From my earliest student days everything that I had attempted had 'come off'. Even this latest, and most difficult, venture into the field of letters had been unbelievably successful."
"Adventures in Two Worlds" by A. J. Cronin

ALWAYS a brilliant student, everything had come to him easily. Despite many hardships along the way, he had at 33 become so successful as a physician that he was planning to move his loving wife and two sons to one of the most fashionable areas of London. But now he was going to give it all up because the doctor said he needed a prolonged rest. He would give it up to become a writer even though he had never in his life written anything other than prescriptions and scientific papers. "Oh, God, you *have* gone crazy," his wife said.

A. J. Cronin, born in Scotland in 1896, was the only son of a devout Irish Catholic father and a Protestant Scottish mother who adopted her husband's faith and had her son baptized into the Catholic Church. This was an insignificant fact in the first seven years of Cronin's idyllically happy and tranquil family life. But suddenly his improvident father died and his mother was forced to move back to the Protestant home of her parents in the west of Scotland where "bigotry was rampant." There the boy was sent to a Protestant school where "my religion brought upon me the jeers of the class and indeed of the master, a sadistic brute who took delight in openly baiting me."

However, as time went on, he grew hardened to this and being skilled at sports, his popularity grew. Always an apt student, it was not long before he won a series of scholarships which enabled him to attend Glasgow University from which he graduated with a medical degree. This was not without its disappointments, however. He was always desperately in need of funds and his heart was set on becoming a surgeon. And so he applied to Sir William MacEwen, his surgery professor and the most noted brain surgeon in Europe, for the menial job of being his "dresser" or "houseman". He had every reason to expect to get the job because he had performed brilliantly on the professor's examinations. But all he received was a polite "no" and the rather imperious statement that "In medicine, or some other field, I believe that you may make your mark. But of one thing I am sure. You will never be a surgeon." Crushed at the time, Cronin in later years would admit that the professor's "unerring judgement never failed him."

He was more successful when he applied for a job as a clinical clerk at the Lochlea Insane Asylum, but that was only because the Superintendent, a Mr. Gavinton, was a football enthusiast and he remembered that Cronin had captained a team he saw play three years before. Throughout the job interview Gavinton talked of nothing but football and when he had exhausted the subject, he turned to Cronin and said "You will report for work tomorrow morning." Then he gave Cronin an advance in pay which enabled him to pay his overdue rent, recover a watch he had pawned and a valise which had been impounded.

His experience at Lochlea was memorable for only one reason—the friendship he developed with George Blair. Blair was a "likeable, gay spirit", an inmate who sang in the church choir every Sunday and played tennis and other games with Cronin. Even though he had been sentenced to the asylum for strangling to death his cousin who Blair claimed had made an attempted attack and rape on his sister, Cronin had become very fond of him.

One night when Cronin was on duty in the absence of the regular doctor, he learned to his amazement and chagrin that Blair had been placed in a padded cell. Puzzled and distressed by this information, he decided to visit with his friend. No sooner had he entered the cell than Blair pounced on him and threw him violently against the door and slammed it shut. Cronin realized now that he was imprisoned with a madman whose state of dementia "rendered his nervous system impervious to pain and excited his muscles to their highest pitch of action, in a padded cell which allowed for no emission of sound or calls for help." He could not hope to overpower such a crazed person. He could only hope that some one would pass by or the old man who had told him that Blair had been confined to a padded cell would remember and think to look for him before it was too late.

He could not remember how long they struggled. He could only remember that Blair had pinned him to the floor and was clutching at his throat trying to strangle him as he had his cousin. Then, as sparks shot before his eyes and his senses began to fade, the door suddenly burst open, and two young male attendants rushed in, threw themselves on Blair and quickly subdued him. Cronin's life had been saved only because an old man had sensed the trouble and then had the good sense to seek adequate help before going to the cell. Cronin himself had learned "never to trust a man who believes he has a sister, when he happens to be the only child."

After graduating from Glasgow University Cronin spent several years serving as an apprentice doctor to a Dr. Cammeron in the rural village of Tannochbrae. Then he obtained employment with the Tregenny Coal Company in South Wales as their full-time medical director at 500 pounds a year and "comfortable living quarters," which turned out to be nothing but a "fourth-rate boarding house." It was to this tattered house and coal mining town that one day in January he took his new bride, Agnes Mary Gibson—who immediately broke into tears at the sight of it. It was so different from "the picture painted by our glowing fancy which, indeed, had envisaged Wales as a land of fruitful pastures and cozy cottages, in short a perfect paradise for two."

Just as they were preparing to retire, there was a knock on the door and a burly Scotsman entered saying, "Hey, mon, be you the new doctor? There's an emergency at the pits, will you come right away?" So Cronin bid his bride of one day goodnight saying he would be back in one-half hour. Little did he realize he would spend the rest of the night 900 feet below the earth's surface saving a miner's life by amputating his leg which had become wedged between the falling rocks.

One year later he moved to another coal mining area, the neighboring valley of Tredegar, as the doctor for the local medical society at the same salary but this time it included a more attractively furnished house. It was here that he made the ambitious decision to study on his own for three major post-graduate degrees to be given by examination through the Royal College of Physicians. Seventy-five per cent of those taking the exams usually failed. In order to prepare himself, Cronin joined the library of the Royal Society in London and had crates upon crates of medical books sent to him. In addition, he was granted four hours off from his practice every Thursday afternoon to go to Cardiff, fifty miles away for two hours work in the biochemistry laboratory of the Cardiff Health Department. In order to gain the two hours work in the laboratory, he had to travel the 100 miles at "breakneck" speed on his second-hand motorcycle, returning to his office at six or six-thirty in time for his night office hours.

At last the day came for the written and oral exams to be held in London. His main concern was not the written part, although a cheap room with "vile" food

at the Museum Hotel was not the most conducive to a
feeling of physical well-being necessary to meet the
stresses and strains of the week-long ordeal. Rather it
was the worry that he would fare badly in the oral part
due to his shabby appearance with his poorly cut suit,
cheap tie and a look of "strained intensity" when he was
measured against all the other candidates, all of whom
were older, more sophisticated, more self-assured and
immaculately attired. Especially when your interviewer
happened to be a handsome, fair-complexioned man of
about sixty, the second most distinguished physician in
Europe, Physician to the King, Lord Dawson of Penn.

Yet when they first met, it seemed to Cronin
that Lord Dawson gave him a look of encouragement,
perhaps because he recalled in his own mind his own
meager beginnings and impoverished youth. Lord Dawson began the questioning:

" 'Can you tell me anything of the history of
aneurysm?' he asked.

'Ambroise Paré,' Cronin answered, 'is presumed to have first discovered the condition.'

Lord Dawson's face showed surprise.

'Why *presumed*? Paré did discover aneurysm,'
he said emphatically.

Cronin's face reddened, then turned pale, but he
plunged on:

'Well, sir, that's what the textbooks say. You'll
find it in every book—I myself took the trouble to verify
that it was in six. But I happened to be reading Celsus,

brushing up on my Latin, when I definitely came across the word ANEURISMUS. Celsus knew aneurysm. He described it in full. And that was a matter of thirteen centuries before Paré.'

There was a long silence before Lord Dawson spoke again. Then he said:

'Doctor, you are the first candidate in the examination hall who has ever told me something original, something true, and something which I did not know. I congratulate you.' "

There was still another day of examinations. When it was all over at four o'clock in the afternoon, Cronin gathered up his coat and prepared to leave, "spent and melancholy", not knowing whether he would be one of the handful (only seven or eight of the original thirty would be accepted) who would receive the great honor or not. As he entered the hall to leave the building, he noticed the tall, imposing figure of Lord Dawson of Penn standing by the great open fireplace in the hall. Momentarily he thought of retreating, but he couldn't escape the steady gaze, then the outstretched hand and the warm smile of the Physician to the King as he beckoned him to his side to tell him the good news. Miracle of miracles, the poor country doctor from a scrubby mine town and not the posh West End of London was now a full-fledged member of the Royal College of Physicians!

But Cronin was an ambitious and determined young man. After three years in Tredegar, during which his first child was born and he was still almost penniless,

he abruptly decided to quit and purchase on time a rundown medical practice in London. It was located in an
area called "Bayswater"—"a rather rundown quarter giv-
en over to boarding houses but near the best residential
districts of the town." In later years, Cronin like to recall
how successful he had been in many different endeavors,
beginning even in his student days. But he worked in-
credibly hard at everything he undertook. In his first
year at Bayswater he didn't take so much as a single half
day's holiday. And, although outwardly he appeared to
be completely reckless with his own career and the welfare of his family as when he would sever all ties with the
past before commencing a new endeavor, it was with dil-
igence and skill that he had prepared himself for each
new opportunity.

One such opportunity occurred late one cold,
foggy November night as Cronin, dressed in his night
gown, sat reading before retiring to bed. The front door
bell rang and when he answered it, there stood a young
maidservant, hatless, coatless and in a great state of agitation. Her mistress, a Mrs. Arbuthnot, at No. 5 Palace
Gardens, had taken poison. She had not been able to
reach their regular doctor; so wouldn't he please come
right away? Without a word he grabbed his medical
satchel, hailed a passing taxi and within four minutes had
arrived at Mrs. Arbuthnot's—still attired in his dressing
gown. There stretched out on a Victorian-style brass bed
lay the frail and all but expired body of an old lady obviously in her seventies—unconscious, with the barest

flicker of life in her faint pulse. Next to her on the bed-side table were two bottles of medicine: one a bismuth mixture for stomach indigestion labeled "one tablespoon as required" and the other, dark blue in color, marked "Liniment—Poison—Not to be taken."

Dr. Cronin quickly realized the old lady had reached in the dark for the stomach palliative and mistakenly taken the near-fatal poison. But what the poison was the bottle did not say and there was no time to call the druggist and get him out of bed to look up the prescription. "The fixed, dilated pupils, dry flushed skin, injected eyeballs, fluttery heart beat . . . and sickly smell of the liniment suggested one thing—belladonna." Belladonna, a powerful depressant, would paralyze the respiratory center of the brain through the vagus nerve and produce the convulsive gasps his patient was now experiencing. But he couldn't be sure—there were at least six other narcotics which could produce the same effects. Still he must make a choice and this was the most likely. So quickly, utilizing all the skills he had learned at Lochlea Asylum, he washed her stomach out with a solution of saline. Next he injected 15 milligrams of diamorphine hydrochloride, the perfect antidote for belladonna, into her veins. All the while he knew that if his diagnosis and ministrations were not correct, at least the treatment would let the poor lady die peacefully and painlessly. There was nothing more that he could do now, but wait.

Fifteen minutes passed in agonizing fear that the worst had already taken place and so there was little hope for recovery. After all, she was old and the poison had already taken its toll on the frail, delicate body before he arrived. Or it could easily be that his diagnosis was wrong and it was not the belladonna that was killing her. All hope began to wane as minutes seemed to be hours and there was not the slightest flicker of life in the aging body. But suddenly her breathing steadied, her pulse became stronger and slowly she opened her eyes. For a long time she just stared blankly at the strange person at her bedside. Then, with a heavy sigh and a glassy look in her eyes, she turned to the good doctor and in a voice barely audible said, "Young man, what are you doing in my bedroom in your dressing gown?"

Thus, in an unknown old lady's bed chamber the "tide gradually turned and began, vigorously, to flow our way." Shortly thereafter Mrs. Arbuthnot's son, Manuel, head buyer for Brunelle's, a fashionable West End shop, called on him and thanked him for what he had done for his mother. Then it was not long before many of the staff of Brunelle's—clerks and seamstresses—became Dr. Cronin's patients; next it was the beautiful models who displayed the extravagantly costly new creations for London's most fashionable women, and finally the socialite customers themselves—"many of them rich, idle, spoiled and neurotic." "Where pence had previously been my recompense, guineas now poured in—a golden stream."

However, despite his great material success, underneath Cronin was uneasy. Once while talking to his wife, he said, "After all, I've come a long way from the days when I tramped up the miner's rows in dirty oilskins and hobnail boots;" to which she replied, "I think I liked you better in those hobnail boots—you thought more of your cases and less of your guineas when you wore them." Cronin reddened but refrained from saying what he thought ("Damn the hell, there's no satisfying you.") Instead he just murmered, "Perhaps you are right."

He had been in Bayswater only five years, but his practice had grown tenfold. He had also been appointed chief medical officer to the great department store, Whitely's, Ltd., and even had been called in on consultation with many distinguished doctors. His two sons were in kindergarten and they were making plans to move to Harley Street, London's most exclusive and prestigious address for the great and near-great of the medical world. Life was good, serene and plentiful.

Then the blow came. On a routine examination for chronic indigestion, a Dr. Izod Bennett, nationally known in the field of digestive disorders, discovered that Cronin was suffering from a duodenal ulcer for which he recommended a special diet and absolute rest for six months. He also warned him that if he did not take care of it there was the likelihood it would perforate and prove highly dangerous.

Cronin considered the possibility of hiring an assistant to take over his practice during his enforced rest, but like many successful men he feared that no one could quite serve in his place as satisfactorily. In fact, he would "ruin the practice in six weeks time," he said. Despite his scientific background and rational mind, Cronin was an impatient and impulsive man who also nursed a secret ambition—to write. Ever since his student days, he had had a "queer urge to be a writer. But naturally if I had told them that back home in Scotland, they'd have thought I was wrong in the head. I had to do something sensible instead. That's why I went in for medicine. It was safe and practical."

For two weeks he said nothing to his wife about his visit to Dr. Bennett. Then one beautiful spring afternoon with the sun streaming into their dining room and their house and the surroundings never looking more attractive, he sat down and told her what had happened. By now he had already sold his practice and made his plans to move away. Confronted with this startling news, Mrs. Cronin turned deathly pale.

"But what are you going to do?" she asked in a trembling voice. Cronin's usual self-confidence for once failed him.

"As a matter of fact . . . I'm going, er, going . . . to try to write," he stammered.

"Oh, God," she gasped, bursting into tears, "You *have* gone crazy."

Cronin tried everything to assuage her feelings with a more detailed explanation of his medical condition and his hopes as a writer saying that if it didn't work out in six months or a year, he would at least "get the bug out of my system." "It's a million to one shot I'm any good," he said. "And if I'm not, I can always come back to the treadmill." But nothing seemed to help. Shock turned to anger as she accused him of not caring for his family and their welfare when he made his decision to give up his practice without consulting them. But words were futile; the crisis resolved itself only when she put her head on his shoulder and "dissolved into tears."

It was a fine June day three weeks later when they arrived at their bucolic retreat, a rented farm on Loch Fyne, a few miles from Inverary in the western highlands of Scotland, midst the windswept moors and mountains of their beloved countryside. As they approached their house, they stopped to savor all of it. "Lambs were frisking in the meadow, a stream, fretted by the sunshine, rippled by the roadside, the children were gathering wild daffodils." Suddenly she was freed from the grip of despair as she threw her arms around his neck and whispered, "It's wonderful to be back again! You'll get well here, dear . . . well and strong. We'll have a lovely time . . . and we'll forget all about that stupid old book!"

But he couldn't forget about 'the stupid old book.' He had told his family that this was what he was going to do, and anything less, in his eyes, would make a liar and a charlatan out of him. Little did he realize the anguish and torment that he would go through in the next three months. Each day he would forego the delights of the countryside—"the sun, the loch, the boat,

the car, the river and the mountains"—to repair to his
attic room armed with twopenny exercise books, a pen,
a dictionary and a thesaurus. Sometimes he would stare
for hours on end at a blank sheet of paper and castigate
himself for his "imbecility" in daring to think he could be
a novelist, a doctor who had written nothing but prescriptions and scientific papers all his life. "What a fool
you are," he would repeat over and over again to himself,
knowing that he had "no pretensions to technique, no
knowledge of style or form. The difficulty of a single sentence staggered me. I spent hours looking for an adjec-
tive. I corrected and recorrected until the page looked
like a spider's web; then I tore it up and started all over
again."

All the while he was reminded of what an old
schoolmaster had once said to him, "Get it down; if it
stays in your head it'll never be anything. Get it down."
And so he did, at first an agonizing, laborious eight hundred words a day; and then, at the end of two months,
as the characters took shape and even came to fascinate
him, two thousand words a day. Sometimes he would
even work into the night or get up in the middle of it,
light a candle—there was no electricity in this remote,
rural area in 1929—in a frantic effort to record a sudden
thought or idea on paper. At such moments, carried away
by his story, he even dared to think he was doing something worthwhile and fine, but "for the most part I felt
that all my drudgery was quite useless, that I was wasting
my time in sheer futility."

This feeling of futility became all but over-whelming the day his first typewritten sheets came back from the secretarial service in London. Then the novel was about half finished, and as Cronin scanned through its first pages he was struck with "horror" by "this awful stuff." Convinced that no one would publish it, he proceeded to take the entire manuscript to the back door where he deposited it into the ash heap. Soon the news of what had happened spread through the house. At lunch no one spoke a word, not even the children. A sense of quiet desperation had taken hold of every one, which no one knew how to break. Finally Mrs. Cronin and their two boys left him to brood on his own. It had started to rain, a slow, steady drizzle, but Cronin decided to go for a walk anyway. Halfway down the lake shore he came on an old farmer named Angus who was "patiently and la-boriously ditching a patch of the bogged and peaty heath which made up the bulk of his hard-won croft."

"When I told him what I had just done and why, his weathered face slowly changed, his keen blue eyes, beneath sandy brows, scanned me with disappoint-ment and a queer contempt. He was a silent man, and it was long before he spoke. Even then his words were cryptic:

" 'No doubt you're the one that's right, doctor, and I'm the one that's wrong . . . my father ditched this bog all his days and never made a pasture. I've dug it all my days and I've never made a pasture. But pasture or no pasture' "—he placed his foot on the spade—" 'I cannot help but dig. For my father knew and I know that if you only dig enough, a pasture can be made here.' "

Nothing more was said. Cronin walked back to the house, "drenched, shamed, furious." Frantically he recovered the now rain-soaked manuscript from the ash heap, carefully dried it out in the kitchen oven and then spread it out on the kitchen table to begin work on it again. It was "a kind of frantic desperation". . . . "I would not be beaten, I would not give in. Night after night, keeping myself awake by sheer will power, I wrote harder than ever." Finally, toward the end of September, it was done. He would describe his sense of relief as unbelievable. Now he didn't care whether it was even good or bad; it was finished, and that was all that mattered—now he could spend the rest of his time fishing, swimming and hiking with his boys over his beloved moors, and act again "like a normal human being."

But first he must submit it to a publisher in London, and he knew of none. Fortunately, a two-year old farmers' almanac which had been left in the farm house had the address of one. So packing the manuscript in an old cardboard box wrapped with ordinary farm twine, he shipped it off, fully expecting a rejection slip for his first effort. Imagine then, the total surprise and elation which greeted the Cronin household when one day in October a wire arrived from the publisher in London saying that they had accepted the manuscript for publication, offering an advance payment of fifty pounds and asking him to come to London immediately. Fifty pounds then seemed like a lot of money and, of course, there would be royalties, he thought. "Pale and rather shaky," he muttered: " 'Maybe, with luck and economy, I can make a living as a writer. Get the timetable and find out when the next train leaves for London.' "

And so it was that Dr. Cronin's first novel, "Hatter's Castle"—"written despairingly"—was published in the spring of 1930. It was immediately acclaimed by the critics and chosen by the Book Society. Since then it has been translated into twenty-one languages, serialized, dramatized and made into a film. It has sold over three million copies. "The flood tide of success was loosed," he said. Even more successful were some of his later novels: "The Citadel" (1937), "Keys To The Kingdom" (1941), "The Green Years" (1944) and "Shannon's Way" (1948). The good doctor had put away forever his stethoscope and his little black bag.

"Though men pride themselves on their great deeds, they are often not the result of design, but of chance."
Duc François de la Rochefoucald

Wilson and Cronin were both ambitious and talented men. Both were frustrated, albeit successful, in their chosen fields of early endeavor—Wilson as a university President which led to the governorship of New Jersey and Cronin as a physician with secret ambitions to become a writer. Neither had any training whatsoever in their final occupation—as U.S. President or writer—in which they proved to be so outstandingly successful.

And both despaired of their chances of attaining that success, Wilson saying "I have not the least idea of being
nominated" and Cronin "I felt all my drudgery was quite
useless, that I was wasting my time in sheer futility."
Each had had minor "Moments" in their early careers—
Wilson when he was apparently "pushed" into the Democratic nomination for Governor of New Jersey and Cronin when he had his successful examination with Lord
Dawson and when he saved the life of Mrs. Arbuthnot.
These moments certainly contributed to the success of
their earlier careers. But if one had to choose a moment
which led to their final fame and fortune—a moment
which, if it had not taken place, would have meant failure, one is forced to think about McAdoo's chance meeting
with Wilson's floor manager, McCombs, which aborted
Wilson's certain capitulation for the nomination, and Cronin's chance meeting with farmer Angus which shamed
him into recovering his rain-soaked manuscript from the
ash heap. Perhaps both would have succeeded without it,
in another struggle, another time. But perhaps not too.

> ". . . *men who persist obstinately in their own ways will be*
> *successful only so long as those ways coincide with those of*
> *FORTUNE; whenever they differ, they fail."*
> *"The Prince" by Machiavelli*

II

THE BIG PLAY

---

1. A MOMENT WITHIN A MOMENT

2. THE MOMENT

ROBERT TYRE JONES, JR.
"I broke through at Innwood."

GAIUS JULIUS CAESAR
"Today you see me either High Priest or an exile."

A Moment Within a Moment

"There's a moment in the life of every moment and God help him who passes that moment by."

TODAY she is the retired reigning queen of the tennis world. But eleven years ago Billie Jean King was locked in an intense struggle for the supremacy of women's tennis with Nancy Richey Gunter. They had not met for $3^1/_2$ years when they stepped onto the court in Madison Square Garden on a winter night in 1968, but Billie Jean wanted this match badly. It was to be her last as an amateur. Nancy had received top ranking in the U.S. in 1964; they were co-ranked number one in 1965 and Billie had received the top honors in 1966 and 1967. However, the last time they had played in 1964 Nancy had scored her sixth victory in seven starts over Billie. Now Billie was out to avenge these losses and enhance her standing as a newly-turned professional.

   Neither girl could know that somewhere in that match, as in all matches between individuals or teams of equal ability, there might be buried one shot, one moment, which would be decisive in the outcome of the match. The fact that they had not played each other for almost four years had not been a studied effort on the part of either girl to avoid the other. It was due more to their completely contrasting playing styles.

Billie, being the aggressive, net-rushing, hard-hitting attacking type, preferred the fast surface of grass on which she had won two Wimbledon titles, one U.S. and one Australian national championship. Nancy's grim, plodding, steady, errorless backcourt game had brought her five U.S. clay court championships, but only one on grass, the Australian in 1967. The Garden court on which they were to play that night favored Nancy, being a slow rubberized composition-type surface. But Billie Jean was determined to have a victory in this her last major match as an amateur. With furious determination, which had become the hallmark of her play, Billie Jean swept her opponent almost off the court in the first set, winning it 6-4, and then going on to build up an almost insurmountable 5-1 lead in the second set. She was only one game away from an impressive victory. But Nancy was not going down without a fight. Summoning all her courage and stamina, she broke through Billie's service in the seventh game and then held on to her own service to make the score 5-3, still in favor of Billie. Now it was Billie Jean's serve and no one in the stands doubted that she could close out the match at will. They played to deuce and finally to match point in favor of Billie Jean.

Then it happened. After a short rally, Billie Jean took to the net and Nancy replied with a weak lob,

normally a sure "put away" for Billie Jean's strong overhead. The match would be over. But no, breaking concentration momentarily, Billie Jean hit the ball a fraction
too late and it landed a foot beyond the baseline. The
score was back to deuce—and then began one of the most
startling winning streaks in Nancy's—or anyone's—tennis career. With the momentum now in her favor, she
not only took the crucial ninth game but every other
game in that set and six more in the final set to close out
the match 4-6, 7-5, 6-0. She had won 12 straight games
against her arch rival. On the final point, a backhand
cross-court which passed Billie Jean at the net, Nancy
lost her usual placid, ladylike demeanor and, exploding
with delight, tossed her racquet high to the Garden's
ceiling. "This was my most satisfying win," she exulted.

One careless error or break in concentration on
the part of Billie Jean King had thus changed an entire
match around, from sure victory to defeat. Sometimes,
however, it is not an error; it might be a brilliant master
stroke at the right psychological moment that determines
the outcome of the match. Such a moment occurred in
the quarterfinals of the 1971 French Championships in a
match between Ilie Nastase, the brilliant Rumanian shotmaker, and America's powerful Stan Smith. Even
though both were established tennis stars, neither had
won a major national championship up to that time. Later that year Smith was to win the U.S. Open at Forest
Hills and, in 1972, the all-England Championships at

Wimbledon. Nastase was to capture the U.S. crown in 1972.

However, on this day the Rumanian had complete control in the early stages of the match winning the first two sets 6-1, 6-3 when the match was called on account of darkness. Resuming play the next day, Smith dominated the action at the outset with crisp, deep, hard-hit volleys from the net, winning the third set 6-3. In the critical fourth set, with the score 4-4 and Smith serving for the game at 40-30, the tall blond Californian hit a deep forehand volley from the net deep into his opponent's corner, a sure winner in most matches. But not against Nastase, who raced to the corner and in a miracle of precision and timing picked it up and shot it narrowly past Smith at the net to land an inch inside the court. It was as if he was saying "if that's best you got, take that!" A dispirited Smith quickly lost the next two points and the match, as Nastase held his own service to win: 6-1, 6-3, 3-6, 6-4.

It was one play alone that turned the tide in the first Super Bowl contest waged between the Green Bay Packers and the Kansas City Chiefs in 1967. The first Super Bowl was also the first confrontation between the winner of the National Football League championship and the American League championship. Fans had argued for weeks, nay years, as to which league was the superior, and Green Bay's narrow defeat of Dallas for the NFL championship that year had not enhanced the older league's reputation. Packer free safety, Willie Wood, was obviously upset when he said "All at once we're too old, overrated and too tired. Well, we'll show them. When we finish, there won't be any doubt that Green Bay is superior or that the NFL is better than the AFL."

After thirty minutes of play and at the end of the first half, there was some doubt. The Packers led the Kansas City Chiefs by a score of 14-10. Actually, the Chiefs had gained more yardage and their quarterback, Len Dawson, had picked the Packers' defense apart as no other NFL quarterback had done during the entire regular season. In fact, Wood himself had looked bad on two of the plays, one of which led to a Kansas City touchdown. During half-time Packer coach Vince Lombardi had taken the unusual step of ordering his linebackers to blitz the passer more often, which was not their usual style of play.

Kansas City received on the second half kickoff and returned the ball to their own 29 yard line. One first down and two plays later they were on their own 49 yard line with third down and five yards to go for the first down—an obvious passing situation. Dawson took the snap and moved back and to the left in a protective pocket of blockers. Packer linesman Henry Jordan and Lionel Aldridge gave chase while linebackers Dave Robinson and Lee Roy Caffey attempted to blitz through to the passer. Meanwhile, tight end Fred Arbanas had cut sharply to the left sideline and was at the Packer 45 yard line, enough for a first down, waiting for Dawson's pass. Dawson spotted Arbanas and let the pass go. But just as he did the pass was deflected and an alert Willie Wood stepped in front of Arbanas and picked the pass off. Quickly a phalanx of Packers moved toward Wood and formed a group of blockers as Wood raced fifty yards downfield to the Kansas City five yard line. On the next play Elijah Pitts burst over left tackle for a touchdown. "We were doing the things we should have been doing," Hank Stram, the Chiefs' coach, said. "Then came that one play. After that, we just broke down." "The interception unnerved the entire Kansas City team," former New York Jet coach, Weeb Ewbank, explained later. Green Bay won 35-10.

The Moment

Robert Tyre Jones, Jr.

"That's why the tournament at Inwood (Long Island) the next year was the hardest of all . . . a sort of crisis . . . if the long lane had not turned at Inwood, I think sometimes it would have gone straight on to its end in the shadows."
Robert T. Jones in "Down the Fairway"

U<small>P TO NOW</small> we have been discussing isolated "moments within moments", certainly decisive within a particular event—moments that gave a player or team the momentum to go on inexorably to victory, but not necessarily critical to an entire career. That such a career-making moment can and does occur is clearly illustrated in the life of the greatest golfer of all time, Robert Tyre Jones, Jr. He was the only man in the history of the game to win the "grand slam" consisting of the U.S and British Open and Amateur titles all in the same year (1930). Jones was always an amateur. Today, in the age of the professionals, the "grand slam" constitutes the U.S. and British Open, the PGA Championship and the Masters (founded by Jones in 1934). Jack Nicklaus has won all of them more than once, but never all of them in one year, nor has any other golfer.

Born March 17, 1902, Bobby was a frail child with digestive difficulties which his father thought would best be served by their moving to the suburbs of Atlanta, Georgia, near the East Lake Country Club. By the time Bobby was 5, Stewart Maiden had become the club's professional golfer, and the family decided to move into a small cottage on the club's property alongside what is now the first fairway. There with the help of Maiden, he took up the game of golf. In later years Bobby was to say he had very little instruction from Maiden but learned the game by imitating Maiden's near-perfect golf swing. Until he was eight or nine his constant companions were not the usual neighborhood playmates a youth would have, but tennis and golf. In fact, he could eat no regular food until he was five years old and the digestive problems continued to plague him until he reached his teens. At nine he had won his first golf cup—the Junior Atlanta Athletic Club Championship, where he played regularly—but he showed no real interest in the game until he was eleven.

Then, in 1916, at 14, he won his first big tournament—the Georgia State Amateur at Brookhaven, Atlanta—which earned him the right to enter the National Amateurs at the Merion Cricket Club in Philadelphia where he lost in the third round to the then national champion, Robert A. Gardiner. He was five feet four inches tall and weighed 165 pounds, a knock-kneed, tow-headed teenager who was gaining as great a reputation for his temper and throwing of clubs with each bad shot as he was with his golf. These tantrums would continue for the next two years. Eventually, he would gain control over the outward manifestation of these tantrums, but never the temper itself which would reveal itself in the redness of his ears.

Eleven years later he would think back to that match and say he had the national champion beaten— even though he was only 14—and then he would wonder if there was not a predestination in the affairs of men and especially in the game of golf. "What was on Bob Gardiner's side that had beat me, and made me blow up, when I was hitting the shots better than he was . . . would it be on my side sometimes—or always on the other side? You know, I never have made sure . . . I found out this much: In the long run it seems to play no favorites—if the run is long enough. In my case it was a run of seven years." It was seven years during which he was to play in eleven national championships, amateur and open, and "still be on the outside."

By 1920 he had grown six inches and lost twenty pounds. After the national amateur in St. Louis in 1921 where he lost in the third round, he came away with a "curious ache in my chest and a definite ache in my left leg . . . suffering from several patches of varicose veins," but the deepest cut of all came when he overheard a golf writer say "sure, he's the greatest shotmaker we have. But he can't win."

The year 1922 was not a good one for Bobby Jones. There was nothing wrong with his mind. He graduated from Georgia Tech with a degree in mechanical engineering and was planning to enter Harvard in the fall to work on a bachelor's degree in literature. The four operations on the varicose veins in his left leg had been successful and again he had managed to win the Southern Amateur championships with "the best-scoring prolonged event I ever played." But something was lacking. The National Championship at Brookline, Mass., again eluded him. "The thorn was beginning to rankle in earnest and . . . I was beginning to brood about it a great deal . . . yes, a great golfer but it's time he was something . . . or was he a great golfer? . . . and a great shotmaker but one who cannot collect the great shots in sufficient numbers to win anything." "What right had I, in the face of almost universal demand, to refuse to be a champion," he would ask himself while admitting that "it was getting on my nerves."

In March 1923 Bobby turned 21, universally recognized as a superb, handsome golfer and as the beau ideal of amateur athletes—one who would never spend more than three months of the year playing tournament golf. The rest of the time he would be studiously preparing himself for a life-time career. Later he was to pass the Georgia bar examination after only a year and a half at Emory University Law School. But for now his golf was known more for its style than its substance. "No one can recall an awkward pose, an awkward swing, a sign of effort beyond control," Grantland Rice, the noted sports writer, observed. Still he had not won a major national championship.

"That's why the tournament at Inwood, Long Island (the U.S. Open), that year (1923) was the hardest of all . . . a sort of crisis," Jones said. After three rounds or fifty-four holes, Jones had a comfortable lead of three strokes. With 18 holes left to play "I had the championship as clearly won as could be." Then he made the mistake, which he never completely conquered, of calculating in his own mind what it would take on the last 18 holes to win the tournament when he should have been concentrating on doing the best he could against "old man par." In later years he would learn to play more against par instead of what other players were doing or not doing, but he never overcame completely "the absolute inability to continue smoothly and with authority to wrap up a championship after I had won command of it." He could only explain this failing by saying that his "singleness of purpose" and "intense desire to win" at the outset forced him to concentrate on playing his best golf, but once he had obtained command "I became fearful of kicking the thing away and began trying to make certain of avoiding a disastrous mistake . . . I was no longer playing the shots for definite objectives."

And this is exactly what happened at Inwood. He finished very poorly, "like a yellow dog," he said, with a 5,5,6 against pars of 4,4,4. As a result, Bobby Cruickshank caught up with him and tied him, necessitating a play-off round. In fact, he had played so poorly he was even glad to have the opportunity to redeem himself in the play-offs. The betting was 10 to 7 on Cruickshank because he had the psychological advantage of having come from behind and presumably had the momentum. As they started, Jones said he felt alright "only sort of numb." For the first six holes he played par golf; yet he fell two strokes behind his opponent who was playing exceedingly well. On the seventh hole, a "tough one-shotter" of 223 yards with a narrow fairway (and a two stroke penalty if one strayed from it), Cruickshank chose to play it safely with an iron which landed short of the green. Jones gambled and went for the green with a spoon and also the chance for a two-stroke penalty which would mean the end of the match for him. But the gamble paid off as the ball came to rest on the green. Cruickshank on his next shot failed to chip dead, missed a ten foot put and Jones picked up a stroke.

By the tenth hole Jones had picked up another stroke and the match was even. Then for the next seven holes the match see-sawed back and forth so that on the seventeenth hole again they were tied, with one hole to go for the championship. Each golfer showed the strain as he teed off on the eighteenth hole. Cruickshank pulled his drive away from the fairway with the ball landing behind a tree on an adjacent roadbed. Jones sliced his to the short rough but on hard, clean ground. Again Jones was faced with the decision, as he had been on the seventh hole, of playing the ball safely back to the fairway in two strokes or risking everything on one shot to the green of about 200 yards. At the seventh he had consciously and deliberately selected the spoon for his shot; this time he would not even remember what he had done. Yet Steward Maiden, his former teacher, would tell him later he had never "played a shot more promptly or decisively." Without any hesitation he picked a No. 2 iron from his bag and "banged" it. All he could remember about the shot was seeing the ball come to rest on the green, dead to the pin, and then, "somebody propping me up by the arm." Then he holed out with a 4 while Cruickshank struggled in with a six. It was Bobby Jones' first national championship. "I don't care what happens now," he said. "I broke through at Inwood."

Later in the year he would lose in the second round of the national amateur championships. "I was disgusted but not hurt," he would say. "I'm going to continue to play in the national amateurs even if I never win one." This was a new attitude for Bobby and he, more than any one, sensed it. He had now learned to play "old man par" in match play and to forget about his opponent—"to save that one little stroke a round that used to get away from me through carelessness or dumb play." "I don't play any better golf than I did five or six years ago . . . all that has been written about my getting control of my temper with better play resulting, is bunk . . . I get as mad as I ever did . . . I don't throw my club away that's all . . . I don't hit the shots any better, and I don't pitch nearly so well as I used to, in the days before I broke through. . . . I simply save that one little stroke a round that used to get away from me through carelessness or dumb play." In the next four years he was to play twenty matches in four national amateur championships, winning eighteen and losing only two of them.

Thus, after seven arid years as an also-ran, it was the famous iron shot—the critical moment—on the eighteenth hole at Inwood which started Jones on the greatest winning streak ever to be played by a golfer. In the next eight years (including 1923) he was to win five U.S. Amateur championships, four U.S. Opens, three British Opens and one British Amateur, including, of course, the "Grand Slam" (the U.S. and British open and amateur titles) in 1930. Jones thought that the "Grand Slam" was more due to "perseverance" than skill and . . . the "decisive factor in each case had been my ability, summoned from somewhere, to keep control of myself and to keep trying as hard as I could, even when there was no clear indication of the direction in which hope of victory might lie." O. B. Keeler, the Atlanta newspaperman who saw him win each of these thirteen major championships, would say: "Looking back . . . you may see crisis after crisis where the least slip in nerve or skill or plain fortune would have spelled . . . ruin. Yet at every crisis he stood up to the shot with something which I can define only as inevitability and performed what was needed with all the certainty of a natural phenomenon."

There may be many "moments" in a person's lifetime, each of which may or may not be met with "inevitability". And each might develop an ebb or flow of its own to create success or failure of a transient nature as in a single tournament or a single match. But they are not the career-making iron shot that Jones made at Inwood. Jones would soon learn to sense these little "moments within moments," as he did in the National Amateurs at the Merion Cricket Club in Ardmore, Penn. on the fourth and last leg of his famous "Grand Slam" in 1930. It would come upon him most unexpectedly in a first round match against the very capable Canadian champion, Ross (Sandy) Sommerville, who later was to become the first Canadian to ever win the U.S. Amateur Championship in 1932. It would be the "real tournament turning point for me," Jones would say.

Up until the seventh hole, a drive and a pitch hole, Jones and Sommerville had about traded strokes though Jones stood at one up. Then each player pitched for about one hundred yards to the green, with Sommerville landing about seven feet to the right of the cup and Jones eight feet also to the right, but with no stymie involved. "There was a chance right here for this match to swing one way or another. Sandy has been hitting right along with me on every shot. On every hole it has been just a question of who would make a putt. I've got the first to go at it this time. If I can get my ball into the hole, Sandy's putt will become a lot tougher and if he should miss, it might mean the match. If I miss first, almost certainly he will hole and we will be even. If that happens, with Sandy in the mood he is in today, I will be playing for my life from here in." The green was "keen" and Jones never worked on a putt any harder than this one. The break from right to left was difficult to read, but Jones gave it just the right touch. The ball hesitated agonizingly on the upper edge of the hole, and then dropped in. Sommerville played the same line, but unfortunately was not as gentle with it and the ball grazed the top of the cup and passed over it by a bare inch. Jones had been right. Instead of being even, he was now two up on Sommerville, with the psychological edge heavily in his favor, as he went on to win the match five and four.

Robert Tyre Jones was certainly the last of the great amateurs and perhaps the greatest golfer of all time, amateur or professional. Before his retirement in 1930 at the age of 28, he had won the U.S. Amateurs five times, the U.S. Open four times, the British Open three times and the British Amateur once—thirteen major tournaments in eight years. And he only played tournament golf three months out of each year, in contrast to today's professionals who play practically the year around. He also had to contend with the wooden shafts of his day each with its own individual characteristics, some fading, some hooking, in contrast to the more stable steel and fiberglass shafts used today.

Jones entire career consisted of only 52 tournaments; the rest of the time he spent as a successful lawyer and businessman. But it was the iron shot at Inwood (and his own character) which had catapulted him into the ranks of the all-time great along with those other legendary figures—Dempsey, Babe Ruth and Bill Tilden—who dominated the golden age of sports between World War I and the Great Depression.

"So what we're talking about is not the hero as golfer but that something Americans hungered for and found: the best performer in the world who was also the hero as human being, the gentle chivalrous, wholly self-sufficient male. Jefferson's lost paragon: the wise innocent."

Alistair Cooke

Gaius Julius Caesar

"I conclude, then inasmuch as FORTUNE is changeable, that men who persist obstinately in their own ways will be successful only so long as those ways coincide with those of FORTUNE; and whenever these differ, they fail. But, on the whole, I judge impetuosity to be better than caution; for FORTUNE is a woman . . . and you will see that she allows herself to be more easily vanquished by the rash and violent than by those who proceed more slowly and coldly."
"The Prince" by Machiavelli
—in praising the actions of Pope Julius II.

IF ROBERT T. JONES took his great gamble with FOR-TUNE with that iron shot at Inwood, it was almost 2,000 years before that Gaius Julius Caesar had taken another kind of a gamble. Historians will tell you that it was when Caesar said "the die is cast" and crossed the Rubicon to crush the forces of Pompey and gain control of the entire Italian peninsula and the Roman state. At the time he was serving as the Governor of Gaul, a Roman province on Italy's northern border. Many times before the Gauls had raided and sacked the Roman towns causing wide-spread panic in the population. But never before had a Roman citizen invaded the Roman state and Caesar knew that any failure would mean that his act of aggression would be considered treasonous. However, with only 300 cavalry and 5,000 foot soldiers he acted with such dispatch and surprise that within 60 days he had struck such terror in the populace, who were reminded of former Gallic attacks, and in the forces of Pompey that they surrendered without a drop of blood being shed. A panic-stricken Pompey declared the City of Rome to be in a state of anarchy as he fled with his army to a place of safety in Greece.

That this was an historical moment and a date to be remembered—49 B.C.—in the life of the Roman Empire, no one will argue. It was a moment from which there would never be a retreat, especially from the dictatorial powers which Caesar set in motion. Thus he became the first undisputed ruler of Rome and the civilized world, a rule he was to exercise for the next five years until his death at the hands of assassins in 44 B.C. But, given his character and talent, it was almost a predestined conclusion—or merely the culminating phase— to a career in politics which had its beginning and its great moment long before.

Caesar was born about 100 B.C. to the aristocratic Julian family, with success in politics seemingly assured because the aristocrats were the only ones who could afford it. Rome was the mistress of the Mediterranean controlling all of Italy, Sicily, Macedonia, Greece and parts of Spain and North Africa. Her power extended to most of the kingdoms of the eastern Mediterranean who looked to her for protection. Her riches from these conquests were so great that in 167 B.C. a law was passed exempting all Romans from paying any taxes. The slaves who had been won either as prisoners of war or sold to Roman families by the pirates performed practically all the work for the wealthier families, thus permitting them to indulge their free time in politics or lavish feasting and entertaining. Slaves ran his house, cooked his meals, worked his farms and even educated his children. And not all of them were engaged in menial work; some were secretaries, some librarians, some even doctors.

For the first twenty-six years of Caesar's life it was not apparent that he had any interest in anything but a life of indolence and pleasure-seeking. In theory, public office was open to any one, but in actuality only the wealthy could afford the vast expenditures for public events and bribery necessary for winning it. "At Rome, all things are for sale," an African chieftain would say as he left Rome after bribing his way out of appearing as a material witness in his own trial.

The public outcry against this sort of thing became so great that one Gaius Marius, the son of a farmer and a plebian, made a name for himself as a champion of the common people. Once he defied the Senate when they tried to curtail the voting rights of the plebians and, in turn, got himself elected consul in 108 B.C. However, the patricians were so powerful and their hold on the Senate so great that Marius would never have been elected had he not married Caesar's aunt, a member of the powerful and wealthy Julian family. Forty years later Caesar would assume Marius' political mantle and become the philosophical and hereditary heir to his uncle's popular political party. Caesar, then, could say like Marius: "They despise me for an upstart, I despise their worthlessness. They can taunt me with my social position; I them with their infamies. My own belief is that men are born equal and alike; nobility is achieved by bravery."

Marius was so popular he held the consulship of Rome six times between the years 108 B.C. and 100 B.C. And it was he who put down the rebellious cities of Italy in 88 B.C. and united the entire peninsula. Unfortunately, his colleague in that effort was one Sulla and Sulla got most of the credit for its success and, as a result, was elected Consul. Sulla, Plutarch wrote, was so ruthless that once after subjugating a rebellious province in Asia Minor "there was no numbering the slain; the amount is to this day conjectured from the space of ground overflowed with blood."

But the power shifted again during one of Sulla's absences from Rome. Marius seized the opportunity and, after forming an alliance with one Cinna, rounded up a band of brigands and freed slaves and massacred

Sulla's followers in the streets of Rome; then had themselves elected co-consuls. This was in 86 B.C. However, Marius died within a few days of his election and Cinna was killed in a revolt within his own camp. In the meantime, Caesar had married Cinna's daughter, Cornelia. And so when Sulla returned to power, he declared all the followers of Marius to be the enemies of the state. Then he set about killing 6,000 of them at one time. Obviously, young Caesar's life was also endangered. Although Caesar was only 17, Sulla decided to test his loyalty by ordering him to divorce Cornelia.

Up to now Caesar had been regarded as a rather frivolous ladies' man and even a dandy who was more interested in the cut of his toga than the fate of Rome. But Sulla's threat of execution if he did not divorce Cornelia was to test his mettle and reveal the raw courage for which he became so well known in later years. Instead of complying with Sulla's order, he fled the city of Rome and took refuge with a few of his slaves in the hill country northeast of the city. Sulla's men were everywhere hunting down fugitives and so Caesar and his small band were kept constantly on the move from one hiding place to another. Once he fell ill from exhaustion during one of his many night marches and his men had to carry him in a stretcher to safety. Another time, ambushed by an enemy patrol, he effected his escape by bribing the captain in charge of it. Eventually he became so weary and discouraged he thought he would go into exile, but about this time he received word that his powerful friends had gone to Sulla to plead for his pardon on the basis that Caesar was just a young hothead and his refusal to divorce Cornelia had nothing to do with the affairs of state. Sulla grudgingly relented but, with great prescience, said: "You have made your point, and you can have him, but always bear in mind that . . . one Caesar is worse than a dozen Mariuses."

And so Caesar returned to Rome. But when a friend offered him a minor position on his staff to fight the rebellious Mytileneans, Caesar readily accepted knowing full well his life would always be in danger as long as he stayed in Rome. Again he displayed his great physical courage and was awarded the coveted civic crown. In 79 B.C. Sulla voluntarily retired from office and one year later he died. Then in 74 B.C. Caesar received word that his mother's brother, Cotta, a Priest, had died in office and that the vacant seat was being held open for him if he would return to Rome. With Sulla's death, Caesar now felt safe in doing so. He was also becoming anxious, now that he was twenty-six years of age, to get started on his political career and such a position, he knew, could lead to the more exalted one of High Priest. He returned and immediately plunged himself full force into the life of politics and that of a politician.

As a Priest Caesar would also become a member of the People's Military Tribune and come in contact with many people and be seen in the Forum every day.

His life would now become that of a typical politician as
he set aside a part of each day just to receive callers and
favor-seekers. To all he showed great courtesy and attention and, as Guglielmo Ferrero, the Italian Historian,
would say . . . "kept a pleasantry or a compliment or a
promise ready on his lips for all comers, invited necessary acquaintances to dinner every evening, put in an
appearance at the marriages, funerals and family festivals
of all classes of citizens, worked in support of some particular candidate in every election that took place, and
gave hospitality in his house or provided regular assistance for a certain number of dependents among the poor-
er classes in Rome who served as his spies among the
people, as his agents during the elections, as a claque
during his speeches in the Forum or as his cutthroats in
any personal quarrel."

The next rung on Caesar's political ladder came
when he was elected one of twenty so-called quaestors or
treasury masters in 68 B.C. This was a minor office but it
carried with it automatic membership in the Senate and
was a very necessary step if one ever expected to become
a Consul of the Roman Empire. The quaestors were assigned to the consuls, praetors and provincial governors
as assistants in charge of their financial affairs. Caesar
was assigned to the province of Farther Spain where in
67 B.C. he traveled throughout the area collecting duties
and tributes from the towns within it. This, in turn, led
to his election two years later to what today would be

considered a foppish position, that of aedile, who was the person who had charge of all public games and festivals. But it was a perfect position in that day for one to build one's popularity and ingratiate oneself with the crowds who had come to expect these lavish displays for their entertainment. To do so, Caesar had to use great sums of money, far more than he had; so he formed an alliance with the richest man in Rome, Crassus, and between them they put to shame all previous attempts that had been made before their time. It was not long before ". . . every one was eager to find new offices and new honors for him in return for his munificence," Plutarch said. Caesar had also succeeded in establishing himself as the political heir to the populist party of his uncle, Marius.

But as Caesar's popularity grew, so did the hostility of the patrician party in the Senate. They knew that the rising upstart would always appeal over their heads to the multitudes to gain his way and that he would be a constant threat to their cherished privileges. The first direct confrontation came when the Senate, led by the great orator Cicero, refused to grant Caesar's friends the troops to secure Egypt and hold it as a Roman province. This was a serious blow to Caesar's prestige. Undaunted, however, he immediately planned a counter-attack. He would run for the highly prestigious office of Pontifex Maximus, or High Priest. Unlike other Roman offices whose term was for only one year, that of the High Priest was for life.

The power of the office lay in the fact that every political action of the state had to be preceded and sanctified by a religious ceremony conducted by the High Priest. Thus it had the effect of giving the office a virtual veto power over every action of the state. Usually it went to a person much older and with greater prestige than Caesar—someone who was either a long-time member of the Senate or a war hero. At 37 Caesar had none of these qualifications. In fact, he was generally regarded just as a somewhat flamboyant but successful politician, heavily in debt for his extravagances but popular with the people. His principal opponent was Catalus Lutatius, long a leading Senator and a man of the highest integrity and reputation.

If Wilson approached the most critical juncture in his career, the nomination for the Presidency, with a resigned sense of fatalism as if it was history's choice and not his which would determine the outcome, it would appear that Caesar had made his choice of the battleground for his future with knowledge aforethought as to its meaning in his career. And he accepted the challenge with a relish and daring which said he was prepared to overcome any and all obstacles in his way to gain it. Up to now each of the public positions he had held had been relatively minor. So he must have known that if he was ever going to succeed on a grand scale he would have to grasp onto a major rung of the political ladder and use it as a springboard for greater things. At times he might have thought of himself as becoming Caesar, the Roman Consul, someday because there were no real limits to his ambition. But this was 63 B.C. and it would be difficult for him to anticipate the long period of apprenticeship that he would serve as Governor of Gaul from 59 B.C. to 49 B.C. And it was inconceivable that his thoughts could have reached out to encompass the military dictatorship he set up after he crossed the Rubicon in 49 B.C. Now, at least, he was more in control of his own destiny—later events would control it—though it meant risking everything on "one turn of pitch and toss" and spending additional vast sums of money.

Even though the odds against Caesar were tremendous, he was counting on two things to work in his favor—the fact that his popularity with the people had grown during his term of office as aedile and the fact that one of his close associates had been able to transfer the power of choosing the High Priest from an antagonistic Senate to a more sympathetic People's Assembly. Thus the fight became a battle between Caesar and the people against the Senate and the established powers. Not only was his eighteen-year political career at stake but also his financial solvency which had been strained to the hilt in previous campaigns. If he lost, it would be virtually impossible for him to regain the credit he would need for any future campaigns. Despite this, he would continue to spend huge sums of money on this one campaign and Catalus, sensing Caesar's financial vulnerability, would offer him a large sum if he would withdraw from the race. Caesar's reply, like that of a riverboat gambler, was that he was prepared to borrow and spend even larger amounts if it was necessary to win the contest.

The day of the election came. Caesar himself would sense the importance of the moment when he embraced his tearful, worried mother and said, rather forebodingly, "Today you will see your son either made High Priest or in exile." But he won and, to everyone's surprise, won quite handsomely. Soon he was settled in the palatial house near the Forum which the state provided for the High Priest. Now he was an established power, and in quick succession other honors and offices were conferred upon him. Within a year (62 B.C.) he was elected a Praetor, one of eight such office holders serving for one year only to preside over the civil and criminal courts. But it was in the following year that he received the most important office of his career when the Senate appointed him to the lucrative office of Governor of Spain. Now he not only had the opportunity to display his innate abilities as a military man but also he was enabled to recoup much of his lost fortune and repay his many creditors. It also brought about a marked change in his character. He was no longer the idle, pleasure-seeking politician presiding over public festivals or ceremoniously sanctioning the acts of others as High Priest. He was a serious and able executive and a first rate military commander who loved to share the hardships of his sol-

diers eating the same coarse food and enduring the same
long marches. Finally, in 59 B.C., as a result of his successful campaign in Spain, he reached the summit of his
powers when he was elected co-consul with Bibulus for
one year (the usual term), thus becoming the top administrative officer of the state, its chief executive and com-
mander-in-chief of the army.

Meanwhile, Pompey and Crassus, both mili-
tary generals, had become two of the most powerful politicians in Rome. But they too were having their troubles
with the Senate, as Caesar would when the Senate appointed him to the insulting post of Superintendent of
Woods and Footpaths. They would also refuse to honor
Pompey's recommendations for the provincial governors
of the Eastern provinces which he had conquered and
Crassus would be denied the appropriations he wanted to
bail out some of his friends who had overbid on their
contracts for the collection of taxes in Asia. Whereupon
Caesar formed a secret alliance with both men and ce-
mented it by offering his daughter, Julia, in marriage to
Pompey. He, in turn, took as his third wife, Calpurnia,
the daughter of one of Pompey's strongest supporters.

When the Senate refused to reconsider the proposals of Pompey and Crassus, Caesar had the measures
brought before the People's Assembly where Cato
sought to speak against them, but was silenced when
Caesar ordered Pompey's soldiers to drive Cato from the
Forum. And when Bibulus wanted to speak against the

proposals, he ordered a bucket of garbage emptied on his head. Both Pompey and Crassus stood by as innocent onlookers during all this. It was now obvious that the secret alliance of Pompey, Crassus and Caesar would sweep everything in its way aside with its strong-armed methods. The alliance was to become known as the First Triumvirate.

Now Caesar had no trouble getting the Senate to reverse itself, withdrawing his appointment as Superintendent of Woods and appointing him to the more exalted position of Governor of Gaul and the eastern Adriatic. He also persuaded them to extend the usual one or two year term of Governor to five years. In 58 B.C. he left Rome for the provinces not to return for nine years. It was during these years and his success in subjugating the rebellious Gallic tribes on Italy's northern border that he gained his reputation as a military genius, which prompted Plutarch to write:

"This love of honour and passion for distinction were inspired into them (his troops) and cherished in them by Caesar himself, who, by his unsparing distribution of money and honours, showed them that he did not heap up wealth from the wars for his own luxury, or the gratifying of his own pleasures, but that all he received was but a public fund . . . added to this also, there was no danger to which he did not willingly expose himself . . . his contempt of danger was not so much wondered at by his soldiers because they knew how much he coveted honour. But his

enduring so much hardship . . . very much astonished them. For he was a spare man, had a soft and white skin, was distempered in the head and subject to epilepsy. . . . But he did not make the weakness of his constitution a pretext for his ease, but rather used war as the best physic against his indispositions; whilst, by indefatigable journeys, coarse diet, frequent lodging in the field, and continuous laborious exercise, he struggled with his diseases and fortified his body against all attacks."

The death of Julia, Caesar's daughter and Pompey's wife, in 54 B.C. and Crassus' in battle one year later set the stage for the struggle for power between Caesar and Pompey. In Caesar's absence Pompey had gained complete control over the most important ruling body in Rome, the Senate. But Caesar had his army and his power base in Gaul and many loyal supporters in the People's Assembly who were calling for Pompey's overthrow. Pompey asked Caesar to return the Legions he had lent him in Gaul. Caesar agreed but asked for a continuance of his command in Gaul and the money to support it. The Senate refused. Other compromises were offered even to the point where Caesar suggested that both men lay down their arms and become private citizens. The people applauded but again the Senate refused, bowing to Pompey's argument that he should not have to give up what was already rightfully his including a new five-year command in Spain.

And so "the die was cast" as Caesar moved his

troops toward the Rubicon River, which formed the southern boundary of Gaul dividing Cisalpine Gaul from Italy proper. There he hesitated, debating long and hard with himself about the historical consequences of his action if he crossed the river. There was no question it would be an act of aggression in complete defiance of Roman law and an invasion of Roman territory precipitating civil war. It was even said that Caesar was so torn that the night before he "had an impious dream that he was unnaturally familiar with his own mother."

Finally, in a "sort of passion" casting aside all caution and calculation Caesar plunged his troops across the river. It was January 11, 49 B.C. Within 60 days he had conquered all of Italy without shedding a drop of blood. He was to be the undisputed ruler of the Roman and civilized world for the next five years until his assassination on the Ides of March in 44 B.C. at the age of 56.

"Genius thrives on conflict and adversity the ordinary man cannot stand . . . the conflict between passion and reason, the irrational and rational . . . the more the average person represses these tensions, the more do they break into anxiety . . . (but) the genius feels the breach of incompleteness until suddenly it is bridged . . . like a flash a new insight springs forth . . . after the most intense concentration . . . (and) he listens to nothing but his own thinking no matter how fanciful it may be."

"Six Who Changed The World," by Henry Enock Kagan.

If Caesar's genius reached full flower when he crossed the Rubicon, it was in essence merely an extension or fulfillment of his already growing power in the state. At this point he was one of the two most powerful men in the state and the only question then was how he would use this power and who would survive. If it had not been the Rubicon it might have been some other circumstance or opportunity he would seize to overcome Pompey and become the sole ruler and dictator. But long before he had faced a more difficult decision when as a lonely, young (37) man he decided to challenge all the ruling powers in the state in his contest for Pontifex Maximus or High Priest. If he had lost, he might have reconnoitered and marshalled his forces to run again for another office and winning, risen to the same prominence. But he was greatly in debt and being a loser, it would have been extremely difficult for him financially and psychologically to regain the momentum so necessary to victory. And so when one reflects on the course of human endeavor, it appears that one has only a fleeting moment—sometimes "a moment within a moment"—and Caesar's was when he ran for High Priest. It was the watershed from which his entire future flowed, first a rapid succession of offices and honors and finally the Rubicon.

III

IMPULSE

ALFRED I. Du PONT

"It is my birthright and I propose to have it."

BOOKER TALIAFERRO WASHINGTON

"The sweeping . . . was my (college) entrance examination."

Alfred I. Du Pont

THE FAMOUS 100 year old family-owned powder-making firm of Du Pont (E.I.) De Nemours was about to be sold to outsiders. This startling news was announced by President Eugene du Pont at a meeting of the family partners in February 1902. The present officers (all Du Ponts) were too sick to carry on and there was no one in the family to replace them, he said. Over in one corner still in his dirty overalls sat the superintendent of the Hagley Yards, a director but not an officer, Alfred I. du Pont, apparently asleep as the minutes of the last meeting were read and other routine business conducted. Some said he snored. He was a family outsider and a man of limited means, but when the motion was made, suddenly he jumped to his feet and declared, "Gentlemen, I'll buy the business." "It's all cash, you know," some one said. But Alfred did not know nor did he have the $12 million they wanted. Yet he bought it.

The first head of the family, Pierre Samuel du Pont de Nemours, was a watchmaker's apprentice who became a liberal philosopher, economist, statesman and

right-hand man to the famous Turgot, French Controller
of Finance. During the French revolution of 1789, it was
only his liberal sentiments that saved him from the guil-
lotine. In 1799 he escaped and sailed for America hoping
to start a social experiment in a colony in West Virginia
called Pontiana. The project failed, but his son, Eleuthère Irénée du Pont—who had dropped the Nemours—
succeeded in another endeavor. Eleuthère had learned
gunpowder making under the French chemist, Lavoisier
and had noted the poor quality of the powder manufac-
tured in America during the frontier days, when demand
was so great. He decided to go into the business and in
1802 he built a plant which was to be called the Eleuthe-
rian Mills on the Brandywine River four miles from the
village of Wilmington, Delaware. Soon his Eagle Brand
powder was the most popular powder available to the
frontiersmen.

Alfred I. du Pont's father, Eleuthère Irénée du
Pont II, was a grandson of the firm's founder. He died in
1877 at 48 years of age from consumption. One month
earlier, Alfred's mother had died in a Philadelphia sana-
tarium apparently of shock when she learned that her
three sons had been beaten black and blue by the nurse
who cared for them during her absence in Europe. Thus,
all five children, with Alfred being the oldest son at 13,
were orphaned. Alfred was born May 12, 1864.

Alfred Victor du Pont (they would call him
Uncle Fred), who lived in Louisville, had promised his

brother, Eleuthère, that he would take care of the children if anything happened to him. But first the older members of the Du Pont clan would hold a family council, as was their custom on all major decisions, to decide not only the fate of the children, but also the house which belonged to the company. Their decision, under the direction of the family patriarch, "Boss" Henry du Pont, was that the children should be placed in homes of other members of the family and the house released to some one else.

But the children had their own ideas and held their own council with the eldest child, Annie Cozenove du Pont, age 17, presiding. And so when Uncle Fred (Alfred Victor) came to their house bearing the bad news, he was greeted not by five suppliant children, but by five heavily armed moppets—Annie with an ax, Marguerite with a rolling pin, Alfred, a twelve-gauge shotgun, Maurice, a flint-lock pistol, and Louis with a bow and arrow. They not only refused to be separated, but also to move an inch from the house. Annie, their spokesman, argued that she at 17 was fully capable of running the house, and that she would finish her own education and see to it that her brothers and sister finished theirs.

Uncle Fred, a bachelor and a successful entrepreneur in his own right as founder of a paper manufacturing company and a horse car line in Louisville, was held in high esteem by the rest of the Du Pont clan and especially its leader, "Boss Henry." So when he presented the children's case to "Boss Henry" (who secretly admired their spunk) and promised to actively supervise them until the girls were married and the boys started in their careers, the family patriarch capitulated. Money was no problem, as Eleuthère had left in trust an estate of approximately $500,000—more than enough for the children's upbringing until they reached the age of 21 when each would receive his share of the estate outright.

"Dupie," as his classmates at Phillips Academy at Andover, Mass. (which he entered in 1879) would call him, did not distinguish himself as a student. He was average in almost all respects. Once he remarked that he got so many 75's because that was the passing grade. If passing had been 85, he would have gotten that, he said. However, he did excell in English and Chemistry and as a flute player, tenor in the glee club and as a general roustabout and mischief-maker who was also handy with his fists.

In the spring of 1882, Alfred finished his studies at Phillips Academy and that fall he continued his lackluster academic career at the Massachusetts Institute of Technology in Boston. He entered as a special student which meant that he took whatever subjects he wanted, but in so doing gave up any hope of obtaining a degree. After an initial attempt at a wide range of subjects—German, chemistry, mathematics, mechanical drawing and forging—his choice of interest narrowed down to just two subjects, chemistry and shop work—perhaps the

two most important to his later career. It was also to
prove significant in later years that he roomed with his
first cousin, Coleman du Pont, from Kentucky, a dash-
ingly handsome young man of towering height (six feet
four inches) who also enjoyed the gay life and turned out
to be the only relative on the Brandywine who could out-
do the five foot eleven Alfred in feats of daring. It was not
insignificant that here too he made the acquaintance of
John L. Sullivan, the world's heavyweight boxing champion, and all-time bare-knuckles champion (1882–1892).
The two men became good friends, Sullivan being attracted to Du Pont's social and educational background,
and Du Pont to Sullivan's great athletic prowess.

Coleman did not return to school in the fall of
1883, choosing to take a job in a Kentucky soft coal mine
owned jointly by his father and uncle (Uncle Fred). Alfred stayed on until the spring of 1884. It was said his
leaving was prompted by the death of another uncle,
Lammot du Pont, who was killed in a plant explosion,
risking his life to warn others of the danger. It had always been a family point of honor to be on hand wherever the danger was greatest, and Lammot had died in
this tradition. As a child, Alfred had loved the kindly
Lammot and considered him the ablest Du Pont of his
generation. And so by the fall of 1884, Alfred I. du Pont
age 20, reported for work in overalls at the lower gate of
the Hagley Yard of the Du Pont Co. as a common laborer at $83.00 per month salary.

For the next twenty-one months he worked at every job in every mill in the company. Finally, cousin Frank (Francis G. du Pont) superintendent of the Hagley and Lower Yards, promoted him from assistant powderman to foreman and then to assistant superintendent at $1,500.00 per year. He liked the work, took pride in it and applied himself far more diligently than he ever had in school. Moreover, he was the only Du Pont to ever share the camaraderie of the other common laborers in the crude club house called "the night shanty", located on the mill grounds. On reaching his twenty-first birthday, May 12, 1885, he became a wealthy young man upon inheriting his share of his father's estate, estimated then at about $100,000.00 Although he continued to work hard, his life style took on a notable change. Instead of always riding a bicycle, he had now acquired a smart looking horse and gig with which he could occasionally be seen taking young girls for rides on Sunday afternoons. He also became a steady patron of the Wilmington Opera House, sometimes escorting a girl, at others a fellow workman from the yards. Often he journeyed to Philadelphia to hear the symphony orchestra or to New York for plays or prize fights, where he would enjoy the company of his old friend, John L. Sullivan.

Henry du Pont ("Boss Henry"), who ruled the firm with an iron hand for thirty-nine years beginning in 1850, died at the age of 77 on August 8, 1889. Son of the firm's founder, he had brought the firm—still a family partnership—to undisputed power and preeminence in the powder-making field. Only one other firm in the United States could even be called a rival, that of Laflin and Rand. Du Pont also dominated the Gunpowder Trade Association whose twelve members made $92^1/_2\%$ of the powder in the United States. The new head of the company would be Eugene du Pont, the older brother of Francis G. (Alfred's immediate boss). Another brother, Dr. Alexis I. du Pont, educated as a medical doctor, but an expert in tram car management, was brought in as a new partner. At the same time Alfred's salary was increased to $6,000 per year, and he was given the active management of the Hagley and Lower Yards, as Frank took on more of the administrative work.

Alfred was not satisfied with his promotion, however; he demanded a share in the partnership. He was joined in his request by Charles I. du Pont, who was the assistant superintendent of the Upper Yards, and Alfred's senior by five years. At first cousin Eugene refused; then reconsidered and offered Alfred a 5% interest, but Alfred said he would take nothing less than 20%, the same amount each of the other five partners had, or 10% for himself and 10% for Charles. The impass was resolved when William du Pont, Boss Henry's son, gave up his 20% and his shares were offered half to Alfred and half to Charles at $225,000.00 each. Charles borrowed the money from William to buy his share while Alfred used $100,000 from his personal fortune; $25,000 which he received as a legacy from the estate of Boss Henry, and he borrowed the rest, or $100,000 from uncle Fred of Louisville at 7% interest.

Thus at 25 Alfred became the youngest member of the partnership and, in fact, one of the youngest in all its history—only four others had been younger, and they had been in the days when the affairs of the firm were far less complicated. But this did not mean that the new partners would immediately become active participants in the decision-making processes of the company. Both tradition and pique dictated against this. After all, Eugene and Francis G. had sat mute throughout the long rule of Boss Henry, and they would expect the newcomers to the company's council to do the same, especially when the young upstarts had brashly forced their way into the family partnership in the first place.

Although Alfred would be ignored in policy-making decisions, he certainly wasn't taken for granted in the yards. There he could perform almost any job any one else could do and displayed a scientific inventiveness which proved most useful to the company, including the invention of a powder press which was the safest on record. However, it was said his greatest contribution was his ability to establish an esprit de corps and enthusiasm among the workmen.

While he had a respectable office in the administrative building along with other company executives, he was rarely either there or in his other office in the

yards, which consisted of nothing more than a chair and
a table in a little stone building in the Hagley Yards.
Most of the time, he could be found among the men in an
open-necked shirt and dirty knee-length knickerbockers
listening to their problems and seeing that the work was
performed correctly. As superintendent, he was all business and could even be brusque at times, but he would
always patiently listen to contrary opinion, weigh the arguments and evidence and then come to a decision. Once
that decision was made, he expected it to be—and it
was—obeyed to the letter, and, unlike others in command posts, he would accept full responsibility for it
whether the results were good or bad.

At the start of the Spanish-American War of
1898, the United States government estimated that it
would need 20,000 pounds of brown powder each day
from the Du Pont company, but the capacity of the
Brandywine yards was only 3,000 pounds a day. Yet Alfred promised he would meet the government's needs
within sixty days. No one thought it was possible, but
by working his men and himself eighteen hours a day
and building new machinery to increase production, to
everyone's astonishment he met the goal.

Despite the predominance of the company in
its field, it was obvious to Alfred and others that it was
falling behind at times. Alfred was especially critical that
they were not rewarding the younger, more vigorous
men, as others such as Laflin and Rand were doing.

Young cousin Pierre, a promising chemist, quit after nine years with the company because he felt that his efforts in the development of smokeless powder had not been properly rewarded. At twenty-nine he decided he would do better with his cousin Coleman in Louisville. Even then, the younger men like Alfred and Pierre were wondering how the waste materials such as wood-tar products from powder-making could be converted to other uses. Alfred had gone so far as to recommend the establishment of a chemical laboratory to study these possibilities.

The three brothers who rejected these ideas and were shaping the company's destiny at that time were either too ill from overwork or old beyond their years. They were: Francis G. du Pont, 49, a good scientific man but a poor manager; Dr. Alex I. du Pont, 56, a fair executive but sick and overworked; and Eugene, 59, the head of the firm, a competent powder man but an inept executive. The fourth senior partner, but inactive in the affairs of the business, was Colonel Henry Algernon du Pont, the best executive of the lot, but more interested in running for the U.S. Senate than he was in the company's business. Of course, the two junior partners, Charles I. and Alfred, were not permitted to have any say in the policies of the company. In 1899 the company was incorporated for two million dollars, a figure far below its true worth. Eugene was elected President, and each of the three senior partners vice-presidents.

Charles Irénée was elected secretary-treasurer and Alfred, nothing—a director only. Outspoken to a fault, Alfred knew his limitations. "I was young, aggressive, and not popular," he would say. "I suppose I was impulsive—and not always polite"—all qualities which would impede his climb up the corporate ladder, but serve him well in the greatest crisis in the company's history.

On January 21, 1902, President Eugene du Pont did not come to work reporting that he had a cold. Three days later pneumonia had set in and on January 28 he died. Immediately the partners held a series of meetings in a fruitless effort to find a successor to Eugene. To none of these was Alred even invited. By seniority Francis G. should have succeeded him, but poor health prevented it, as it did for Dr. Alexis. Col. Henry Algernon du Pont, deep in a campaign for the U.S. Senate, excused himself, and Charles I. was both too young and in poor health himself. No one even considered Alfred, although he was probably eliminated on two counts—too young (38) and too impulsive. Thus, the senior partners came to the conclusion that they had no alternative but to sell the business outright.

It became Frank's lot to break the news to Alfred, which he did, saying there was no one to run the business and therefore, they had decided to sell it, suggesting that Laflin and Rand would be the most likely purchaser. For once, Alfred held his tongue despite his inner revulsion to the idea of selling one of America's great industrial enterprises, controlling one-third of the U.S. powder market, which had been in the same family for five generations. He simply replied that under the circumstances "a disposal of the assets of the company seemed advisable." But he took the next train to New York to see his bankers about a possible loan in case it became necessary to stop the sale to Laflin and Rand. Later, continuing the subterfuge, he was to tell members of the family he was thinking of going to France to learn the automobile manufacturing business, and when some one said to him: "You couldn't run the business, could you?" He replied, "No, maybe I can push a wheelbarrow, but that's all the sense I have."

In February 1902 the fateful stockholders meeting was held; it being a foregone conclusion that each of the five partners had decided the company must be sold. It was also the first meeting in years that Alfred had attended, and he made no effort whatsoever to observe the proprieties of the situation, appearing in his grimy work clothes laden with smoke powder and dirt. There were reports that he slept and even snored through the reading of the minutes by Secretary Charles I.—at best he took on an air of complete disinterestedness and sat with his eyes closed.

One by one each stockholder apologized for his inability to carry on the business, mostly pleading poor health and with some justification—Charles I. was to die within the year, and death for Alex I. and Francis G. was

only two years away. The only healthy ones were cousin
Col. Henry Algernon du Pont, still occupied with his
running for the U.S. Senate, who didn't want it anyway,
and Alfred I., something of a family rebel who was too
erratic and outspoken to be considered. Thus, a business, started 100 years before with $36,000 capital by
Eleuthère Irénée du Pont on the banks of the Brandywine and carried on by three generations of sons and
grandsons, now worth, according to its present owners,
at least $12 million, was to be put on the block and sold.
No one could anticipate that within two years (1904) its
net profits alone would amount to $4 million and that
within a year after that, the Du Pont company would
control two-thirds of the U.S. powder market. It was
Col. Henry who made the motion to sell and suggested
that the most logical purchaser was its principal com-
petitor, Laflin & Rand. He also suggested that Hamilton
M. Barksdale, a brother-in-law to Charles I. du Pont, be
appointed to negotiate the sale for at least $12 million.

So far the meeting had been one of complete
decorum and agreement. And no one was greatly disturbed when Alfred I. slowly opened his eyes and quietly asked that the motion be amended to provide that the
company be sold only to the highest bidder. Col. Henry
and the others readily accepted the motion as amended
and the meeting was adjourned. Whereupon Alfred
jumped to his feet and declared "Gentlemen, I'll buy the
business!" As every one sat in shocked silence, the im-

pulsive young man moved toward the door as if to defy any one to leave, saying again "Yes, I'll buy the business."

Cousin Frank was the first to regain his composure pointing out that he could not buy the business because "it's all cash, you know." With this all the pent-up emotions of the eldest son of the eldest son of the eldest son of the eldest son of the founder of E. I. du Pont de Nemours & Co. broke loose. "Why not," he replied in that high, shrill voice which was typical of him when he became excited—"if you can't run the business sell it to some one who can." Then he launched into a tirade against the present managers and charged that the predicament of the company was due to their failure to recognize the ability of the younger generation and give them more responsibility. "By all rights of heritage, it (the business) is my birthright; I can pay as much as any one else and I propose to have it," he shouted. Finally, the old warrior, Col. Henry slowly rose from his chair, placed a hand on Alfred's shoulder and said "All right, I am with you. Gentlemen, I wish to say this has my hearty approval. I shall insist that he be given the first opportunity to acquire the property." With this the meeting was adjourned. Alfred was given one week to raise the money.

Thus, at 38 years of age, out of sheer impulse, resentment towards his elders and pride in family ownership, the young yard foreman had undertaken to buy a

multimillion dollar enterprise with only the vaguest no-
tion as to where the funds were coming from and even
less of what the true value of the business was. Certainly
the other stockholders did not take Alfred's offer serious-
ly. Immediately after the meeting Dr. Alex got in touch
with the proposed negotiator, the able Hamilton M.
Barksdale, a Virginian who had married the sister of
Charles I., and not only offered him the Presidency to
better conduct the negotiations, but said he could continue indefinitely, if the sale could not be accomplished.
Only in passing did he mention Alfred's offer to purchase
it. But Mr. Barksdale declined, saying he thought all efforts to obtain some one with the du Pont name to man-
age the business should be exhausted first.

      "For many years before it came in 1902 I had
been preparing for a crisis in the affairs of the company,"
Alfred was to say in later years. Now it was upon him
and he was ready. First he got in touch with his old
roommate and cousin, the flamboyant, bold, confident
Coleman (Coly) du Pont who had been so successful in
the mining and streetcar business in Kentucky. He was
his first choice to run the business. Next was another
cousin, the quiet, unobtrusive Pierre du Pont, a chemist
with a flair for corporate financing, who had quit the
company four years before when his work in developing
smokeless powder went unrewarded. Now 29, he owned
a successful streetcar business in Lorain, Ohio.

      Even Coly was shocked by the magnitude of
Alfred's offer and begged to confer with his wife, Elsie,

before reaching a decision. Elsie's only comment was "You know what it is like to be in business with your relatives." "Then I won't go in unless I have a free hand," he assured her. Whereupon he telephoned Pierre in Lorain and said he would go in if Pierre would and both agreed to meet at Alfred's house, "Swamp Hill," in Wilmington, Delaware to talk it over.

When they met, Coleman demanded a free hand in the management and a lion's share of the stock in a new corporation they proposed to set up to buy the business with. Alfred and Pierre raised no objections. On the question of what they should pay for the business, none had the slightest idea of its true worth, although they were all agreed that its value lay somewhere between twelve and twenty-four million dollars. Little did it matter, it was decided, as long as the present owners were thinking in terms of twelve million and the only cash outlay the buyers planned to make was $700.00 apiece. This represented each buyer's share of the twenty-one shares of incorporators' stock in the new company at a par value of $100.00 per share. Coleman was chosen as their spokesman to meet with the family elders to negotiate the terms, but like any good promoter he was not going to use any of his own or partner's cash if it could be avoided.

"You wouldn't want to cripple our plans by tying up all our cash," he told them as he offered them $12 million in purchase-money notes at 4% interest plus a bonus of stock in the new corporation, depending on a

final determination of the value of the assets of the old
corporation. The next day Eugene du Pont, Jr. told
Pierre in confidence that the family elders had accepted
the proposition presented by Coleman.

And so Pierre dropped around the office, hoping to get an inventory of the assets. There he found
Frank, who was the acting President, sitting at his desk
opening the mail. He mentioned to Pierre that there were
some matters that needed his immediate attention. But
Pierre put him off saying that he and his cousins were not
prepared to take over yet, that nothing was even in writing and that the purchase price was yet to be settled.
"These are just details," Frank replied as he put on his
coat and hat and prepared to leave. A stunned and
speechless Pierre watched as Frank left the office saying,
"The elders have decided to sell and that's that."

Thus, on March 1, 1902 the three cousins took
over one of America's largest business enterprises without so much as one dollar exchanging hands. In later
years when Pierre was asked why they would pay the
seller's asking price of $12 million without taking an in-
ventory of the assets, he replied it was because of "the
character of the sellers." Whatever else might be said, the
integrity of the Du Ponts was unimpeachable.

The final price arrived at was $15,360,000 con-
sisting of $12,000,000 in purchase-money notes at 4%
and $3,360,000 in 33,600 shares of stock in the new com-
pany with a par value of $100 each. The total number of

shares issued by the new company was 120,000 which left 86,400 shares to be distributed among the three cousins as promoters' profits. Coleman, as President, received the lion's share, or 43,200 shares; and Alfred as vice-president and general manager and Pierre as treasurer, each got 21,600 shares. Therefore for an expenditure of $700.00 each, Coleman got stock valued at $4,320,000 and Alfred and Pierre each received stock worth $2,160,000. But this was just the beginning. Within two years net profits alone were $4,000,000 and within ten years they were $7,000,000, or almost half the purchase price of the company.

The three heads of the firm were chosen well by Alfred. They made a perfect combination. Some one described the six foot four Coleman as "a giant of a man, with the head of a hawk, mind of a Medici and a frontiersman's lust for conquest." Alfred's sole interest and love was the operational side of powder-making, in which he excelled, and Pierre, aided by a bright, young stenographer named John Jacob Raskob, whom he brought into the company, proved to be the financial wizard.

At the time of the purchase, the Du Pont company owned a minority interest in eighteen other explosive companies; Laflin & Rand had a minority interest in seventeen. Within two years, Du Pont had gobbled up Laflin & Rand and controlled 56% of the powder-making production in the United States.

It was the day of the big trusts in America and the zenith of Alfred's success in the company. In fact, by 1905 they had cornered 75% of the market. Coleman's drive and acquisitiveness, Alfred's productive genius, and Pierre's financial wizardry and soundness produced the first company dividend in 1904, 50¢; in 1905 it had risen to $3.50; $6.50 in 1906 and $7.00 in 1908. And yet even with these enormous distributions, the company in 1907 had accumulated reserves in excess of $10 million— a tribute to the basic conservativeness of its financing.

Today, of course, it is no longer the $15 million business devoted strictly to powder-making which Alfred had saved for the Du Pont family, but rather America's largest chemical and synthetic fiber-making company worth perhaps $10 billion. But Alfred and Coleman's stars were to shine only briefly. Within nine years Coleman had taken a leave of absence as President, owing to illness, never to return, and Alfred had been ousted as operational manager.

Alfred's difficulties were mostly of a personal nature. He and Bessie were divorced in December 1906 and in October of 1907, he married Alicia Bradford Maddox. For no apparent reason Coleman took a critical view of all this and, in fact, tried to buy Alfred out saying "Don't you think you'd better sell out to me and get away from here?" Alfred refused, but a family rift of serious dimensions developed from it. The breach was further widened in 1910 when Coleman and Alfred tried to buy the same piece of land in Brandywine, and Coleman got it. Then a year later, Coleman got hold of some letters concerning the marital difficulties of Alfred's daughter, Madeleine, and sent them to Alfred. Alfred returned them to Coleman unopened saying curtly they were a private matter for the person addressed and not for either Coleman or himself to pry into.

About this time Coleman took his leave of absence and Pierre was elected acting President by the Board of Directors. Gradually Alfred's personal relations with the other Du Ponts worsened and even reached the point where he filed a slander suit against them for their personal attacks (never explained) against his second wife. Eventually the suit was dropped, but Alfred, as if to show them all, then started building his now famous "Nemours" estate outside Wilmington for his wife, at a cost of $2 million and twenty years' work. In January 1911, the Executive Committee, under Pierre as acting President, approved a reorganization plan which relieved Alfred of his operating duties as general manager. Charles' brother-in-law, H. M. Barksdale, took his place. Alfred remained a vice-president and member of the finance committee, but without any duties. However, the company continued to prosper and in each year from 1910 through 1912 paid the huge dividend of $12.00 per share. Alfred's income from these dividends was $400,000 per year. He was 47 years of age.

In February 1915, due to his illness, Coleman offered to sell all the stock he owned to the company. He wanted the going price of $200 per share. Alfred didn't

think the company should pay over $125 per share. So
Pierre went off on his own and, with some degree of duplicity, organized the Du Pont Securities Company
which borrowed the $14 million from J. P. Morgan Co.
and used Coleman's purchased shares as collateral for the
loan to buy Coleman's stock. Thus Pierre got 50% of
Coleman's stock and the rest was divided between Irénée, Lammot and Felix du Pont. Ruby Carpenter and
John J. Raskob each got 5%. Immediately, Alfred,
Francis I., Philip and others sued the Securities Company and Pierre personally for defrauding the company.

Although Alfred had done much the same
thing in buying the company in 1902, the purpose of his
action then was above reproach—to save the company.
Now the purpose of Pierre's financial legerdemain, Alfred argued, was solely to acquire Coleman's shares
which the company should have bought in the first place.
Alfred's motives had served him well in 1902; in 1915
they failed him completely, as he was too trusting of others.

Also he grossly miscalculated the value of the
stock if he thought it was worth only $125 per share.
World War I had started in Europe and Du Pont had become a major supplier to that market. Seven weeks after
the transaction, the stock rose to $300 per share and by
late August it was $700. Then in September of 1915, the
original E. I. du Pont de Nemours Co. stock was split
two for one and the new stock jumped to the equivalent
of $900 per share of the old stock. So in less than one year
the stock had gone from $200 to $900 per share and the

dividends paid during that year amounted to $82 per old share. Alfred's dividend income from his Du Pont stock alone amounted to a whopping $3,000,000 in 1915.

On January 10, 1916 the blow fell. Pierre asked the Board of Directors to depose Alfred from his position as vice-president and as a member of the finance committee. The motion carried by a 13 to 1 vote, with Francis I. casting the lone dissenting vote. Twenty-one months later he was struck again. Although in the spring of 1917, the lower court had taken note of Pierre's duplicity in obtaining Coleman's stock through the facade of the Delaware Securities Co., it ruled that the stockholders themselves should vote on whether the company or Pierre and his friends were entitled to it. In October the vote was taken and Alfred lost by better than a two to one margin. Alfred wanted to drop the suit, but his friends persuaded him to appeal it. The appeals court not only upheld the lower court, but exonerated Pierre of all wrongdoing as an officer of the company.

Thus at 53, after nearly thirty-three years with the company, the still young and vigorous erstwhile savior of the family fortunes, powderman, musician, inventor—"the most brilliant, diversified and accomplished Du Pont of the time"—would have his last remaining ties to the company severed irrevocably. While still a major stockholder, until his death in 1935, he would not even be asked to serve on its Board of Directors.

There would be other successes—in banking and land development ventures in Florida where in 1926 he transferred most of his holdings and assets—and

one major failure. This was a trading company in
New York which he organized toward the end of World
War I to help war-torn Europe and in which he was
bilked out of over $5 million by its managers. Measured
on a monetary basis, he was four times as successful as
his first cousin, Coleman, who always prided himself on
his ability to make money. When Coleman died in 1930,
he left an estate valued at $17 million. And the Great
Depression of 1929–1932 had reduced Pierre's worth to a
point where it was about equal to Alfred's because Alfred
had had the foresight to see it coming and had converted
large amounts of his holdings into cash. In fact, at the
peak of the 1929 stock market, Alfred was reputed to be
worth $120 million.

But none of this meant very much to the man
whose courage and good instincts had brought such great
monetary rewards to himself and his two cousins. His
years of real success, when he was a power and force in
the company, had been all too brief, dating from that
moment in 1902 when he barricaded the door of the
Board Room with his large frame and declared "I'll buy
it" to that day in 1911 when he was relieved of his duties
as the operating head of the firm and "kicked upstairs" to
a vice-presidency—a period of only nine years.

On the day of his retirement the men with
whom he had worked in the yards voted to give him a
silver cup. At the presentation ceremonies Frank Pyle
read the resolution which said in part "we have hereby

resolved that we feel keenly the loss of our leader and chief . . . (whom) we have always found a friend." To this Alfred replied, "Some men measure their success with the wealth they have attained; others have political ambitions, and so on. I, myself, have always believed that the man most to be envied was he who, through life, has won the love and esteem of the greatest number of his fellow men . . . with (you) I began my life work and for years we have toiled as brothers, through days of sunshine and days of sorrow. You may, therefore, feel assured that no gift of the past or the future will be as greatly cherished as this exquisite token that you give to my keeping."

Booker Taliaferro Washington

From the Census of 1860

The Slaves of James Burroughs: Franklin County, Va. 1860.

Names of Slave Owners	Number of Slaves	Age	Description Sex	Color
Jas Burroughs	1	41	F	B
	1	40	F	B
	1	22	M	B
	1	12	F	B
	1	8	M	M
	1	4	M	M
	1	1	F	B

THE ABOVE is the first recorded document of the existence of one Booker Taliaferro Washington: a slave, age 4, male, mulatto. Son of a house servant and an unidentified white man, he was born about April 5, 1856 as a slave on the James Burroughs farm near Hale's Ford, Virginia. He was known then only as "Bowker", and one year later he was so listed in an inventory of the estate of Mr. Burroughs and given a value of $400, along with such other items as:

1 Lot Scantling & Plank	$1.50
Shovel Digger & 3 Forks	1.00
5 Turning Plows & 3 double Trees	10.00
7 Hilling Hoes, 3 Grubbing Hoes	2.50

There he remained as a slave until freed by the Civil War, living with his mother, brother and sister in a 14 ft. by 16 ft. log cabin and sleeping on a pallet of dirty rags laid upon a dirt floor. He was to receive no schooling as long as he was a slave, which was about to the age of nine. Yet he would grow up to become one of America's greatest educators, the founder of the now famous Tuskegee Institute in Macon County, Alabama.

No one had a more miserable youth. All through his boyhood years, during which he didn't even have a surname until it was required by his attendence in school, he labored in salt and coal mines. Later he wrote that not once did the entire family sit down at a table together for a meal. Meals were gotten "much as dumb animals get theirs" . . . "a piece of bread here and a scrap of meat there." There were no utensils to eat with, only their bare hands.

After the war, his stepfather, who had been a slave of another owner and was now freed, found his way into the new state of West Virginia where he settled in Kanawha Valley in a town called Malden which was about five miles from the present state capital of Charleston. Then he sent for Booker and his mother who made the trek of several hundred miles from Alabama mostly on foot, although they had a cart and horse with them to carry their meager belongings. There he went to work with his stepfather in the salt mine, going to work at 4 a.m. every day. He obtained his "first learning" in the mine when he learned to recognize the number "18", the number of his stepfather's salt barrel. Despite the "drinking, gambling, quarrels, fights and shockingly immoral practices" of a mining town, young Booker was determined to get an education. "I recall," he said, "that I had an intense longing to learn to read" . . . and "I determined I would get enough education to enable me to read common books and newspapers."

His mother and all the other negroes in the area were illiterate, but somehow she was able to obtain an old Webster's blue-back spelling book and from it Booker taught himself the alphabet. One day a young negro "with considerable education" came to Malden and each colored family agreed to pay him so much a month so that he could "board around" and give their children the rudiments of an education. At that time there was no school in the area. Later there was, but Booker's stepfather would not let him attend it because he said the boy was too valuable to him in the mines. Booker was terribly disappointed, and so his mother arranged to have the teacher come to their cabin at night to give him his lessons. Booker was still dissatisfied because what he wanted so much was to go to regular school in the daytime. Finally they reached a compromise that if Booker would work in the salt mine from 5 a.m. until 9 a.m., when school started, and again after school until the mine closed, he could go to school with the other children. But the strain of such long hours soon became so great and his attendence at school so irregular that he was forced to give the school up. The result was that he received most of his boyhood education at home at night.

Later on work was secured for him in the coal mine. This he soon learned to dread—not only the back-breaking work, the dirt and grime, but especially the fearsome mile-long trek in the darkness from the opening in the mine to the face of the coal where they were working. Oftentimes he would find himself envying the better lot of the white boy, but he would quickly cast the thought aside by telling himself that "success is to be measured not so much by the position one has reached in life as by the obstacles which he has overcome while trying to succeed."

One day while at work he overheard two miners talking about a great school for the colored somewhere in Virginia. Stealthily he crept forward so as not to disturb them but to hear better what they were saying. He was sure he heard one of them say a student didn't need money to go to this school. He could work out all or a part of his expenses and at the same time learn a trade or business. Then and there "I resolved to go to that school." And the thought of how to get there was with him day and night although he didn't have the faintest idea as to where the school was or how he would ever get there.

He continued to work in the coal mine a few months longer until one day he heard there was a vacant position in the household of General Lewis Ruffner, the owner of the salt and coal mines. The vacancy occurred because no one would work for the very demanding, meticulous Mrs. Ruffner, a Vermont woman who was also a very strict disciplinarian. Booker's mother applied for the job for him anyway and he was hired at $5.00 per month as a houseboy. He soon learned that she wanted everything kept immaculately clean, the work done promptly and systematically and that she insisted on absolute honesty and frankness. Others had lasted only two or three weeks on the job; Booker was to remain with her for one and one-half years. He was now of high school age and Mrs. Ruffner encouraged him to continue his studies, letting him off for one hour each day during the winter months to go to school. However, he continued to receive most of his education at night from a teacher who was paid to come to his home. In later years he would feel that "the lessons I learned in the home of Mrs. Ruffner were as valuable as any education I have ever gotten anywhere since."

Most of his pay he gave to his stepfather, but he was able to save just enough so that in the fall of 1872 he took the first step in his life-long ambition to attend the Hampton Normal and Industrial Institute in Hampton, Virginia. This was the school he had heard his fellow miners talk about years before in the mines. It was 500 miles from Malden, a long journey for a young man with very little money in his pocket. He got as far as his money would take him by stage coach. Then by walking and begging rides he reached Richmond, Virginia, 82 miles from Hampton, arriving there at midnight, tired, hungry and without a penny in his pocket. For a long time he just walked the streets, not knowing what to do nor which way to turn until finally he came upon a wooden boardwalk which had been built well above the ground level. It was now dark and he didn't know what else to do; so he crawled below the boardwalk and made this his bed for the night. He didn't know it then, but this was to be his bed and home for many nights to come. The next morning he walked down to the harbor and there noticed a large ship unloading its pig iron cargo. He asked to captain if he could help in the work of unloading, and the captain said he could. In this way he earned at least enough money to buy his breakfast and food for the next several days but not enough to pay for a night's lodging anywhere. Anything extra he made he knew he had to save for the rest of the trip. So the boardwalk and the stars continued to be his home as long as he was in Richmond.

Finally he had saved enough to continue his trip to Hampton, which he did, arriving there with only 50¢ in his pocket—an unwashed, smelly sixteen year old boy with clothes in tatters seeking admission to the now famous Hampton Institute, founded in 1868 by General Samuel Chapman Armstrong. There he sought out and was interviewed by another meticulous and proper "Yan-

kee" woman known as the "head teacher", a Miss Mary
F. Mackie. Miss Mackie could only have been shocked,
to say the least, and even repelled by the appearance of
this young man who was seeking admission to their college. It was not only his appearance that disturbed her
but the fact that he had had practically no formal education and what he did have was gained in snatches between shifts in the coal mines or at night with an unknown teacher. It was no wonder that she put him off
day after day until finally, out of pure compassion, she
asked him to clean out the recreation room. At least, she
thought, the boy could earn enough to buy a regular
meal.

No one worked harder in cleaning that room
than Booker T. Washington, using all the experience and
skill he had learned in working for Mrs. Ruffner. He
swept it out three times, scrubbed it, dusted everything
four times, cleaned the windows until they squeaked.
Then he went over everything again another four times,
including all the woodwork, tables and desks! It was now
late in the day and everyone had gone to their rooms to
await the dinner call. All alone in the dread stillness, a
nervous boy awaited Miss Mackie's inspection and verdict. Finally she came. Without saying a word she
walked around the room looking into every nook and
cranny for dirt, and "being a Yankee woman . . . (she)
knew where to look for dirt." Then she took out her
handkerchief and started to rub it over the woodwork

and along the furniture and even on the floor. At last when she had finished and Booker could see that she could find "not a particle of dust", she turned to Booker and said with just a trace of a smile "I guess you will do to enter this institution." Later Washington would write: "I have passed several examinations since then, but I have always felt that this was the best one I ever passed."

Certainly it was the most important moment in the life of this ex-chattel slave in his rise to become one of America's foremost educators. It was the precise moment from which everything else in his life flowed—his own education and his subsequent preeminence in the educational world. Had he failed, he too might have been just an obscure number "18" in the dark reaches of some nameless coal or salt mine somewhere for the rest of his unremembered life. Perhaps young Washington at 16 didn't even realize the full significance of cleaning that room or its consequences or what would happen to him if he didn't do a superior job. But the fact remains all his training and ambition came to bear on this one task and the result was the fulfillment of his great desire for an education.

And so Booker T. Washington was hired on as a janitor, which was enough to pay for his room and board of $10.00 per month. His tuition of $70.00 per year was donated by a Massachusetts gentleman at the request of the school's founder and principal, General Armstrong, who later took a special interest in Washington and guided his career until his death in 1893. For a long time the boy was so poor he had only one pair of socks, which he would wash over and over again as they became soiled. He began his janitorial duties after classes each day and worked until midnight, rising at 4 a.m. the next morning to do his studying for that day's classes. He graduated in June 1875 and that fall he returned to Malden where he secured a teaching position in a colored school.

Four years later he was asked to return to give the commencement address at Hampton. Evidently the speech pleased every one and later that summer General Armstrong asked him to return in the fall to teach part-time and continue his educational pursuits. Then in May 1881 General Armstrong asked him if he would like to take charge of a colored normal school in Tuskegee, Alabama.

The Alabama legislature had appropriated $2,000 to the school for teachers' salaries, but for nothing else. There was no money and no appropriation for money for buildings. When Washington found out about it, he said it "left me with a heavy heart . . . I was only one person, and it seemed to me that the little effort which I could put forth could go such a short distance toward bringing results. I wondered if I could accomplish anything, and if it were worthwhile for me to try." Tuskegee, the county seat of Macon County, was then a town of only 2,000 people located in southeastern Alabama near the state capital of Montgomery. It was in the heart of the Black Belt with half of its people being colored.

But both the colored and white people of Tuskegee were interested in starting the new school for the training of Negro teachers, and Washington was not one to back away from a challenge no matter how great. Finally he located an old "shanty" next to the colored Methodist Church and announced that July 4, 1881 would be the opening date for the new school. Washington had decided that he would take no one less than 15 years of age or without some educational background. And so the first class numbered 30 students ranging in age from 15 to 40. The building was so dilapidated that when it rained, the students would hold an umbrella over Washington's head while he continued to teach. By the end of the first month, the enrollment had increased to fifty. And within three months, he was able to acquire for $500.00 a tract of land of 100 acres one mile outside Tuskegee which had been an old plantation. To do this, he had borrowed $250.00 from an old friend in Hampton.

The main house of the plantation had burned to the ground, leaving only a cabin, an old kitchen, a stable and a hen house. Washington knew that his students, who were used to living in the crude cabins of the cotton, sugar and rice plantations of the south, would not expect to have luxurious quarters. But he also knew that they would appreciate it more if they had helped in the construction of the buildings with their own hands. And they would learn something about the building trades as they did so.

It was this philosophy together with the dynamic leadership of its founder which has made Tuskegee Institute the dazzling success it is today. Now, almost 100 years later, it has 159 buildings valued at $14 million located on 4,935 acres of land, a library of one million volumes, an endowment of $13 million, an annual budget of $4 million and a full-time faculty of 226, fully accredited by the Southern Association. Its proudest boast is that a Negro, George Washington Carver, taught there and conducted his famous experiments which led to the discovery of hundreds of uses for the peanut, soybean and sweet potatoe—all because at one time a 16 year old boy cleaned a recreation room so thoroughly.

IV

IMPULSE
AND
DETERMINATION

SARAH BERNHARDT
"Quand-Même (despite all)."

ANNE SULLIVAN MACY
"There is . . . something within us . . . some innate capacity . . . we did not know . . . until the hour of our great need brought it to light."

Sarah Bernhardt   Anne Sullivan Macy

ONE WAS the illegitimate daughter of a young French milliner and her lover, a struggling lawyer. The other was the victim of such poverty and disease that she was nearly blinded when she was three by trachoma of the eyes. The first was deserted by her father and left by her mother to be raised by a nurse in the slums of Paris. The mother of the second died before she was nine and her father, a common laborer, deserted her and left her to be raised by his cousin, the most prosperous of the Irish Sullivans living near Feeding Hills, Massachusetts. Yet both were so impetuous and strong-willed that they broke even these slender bonds of security within a few years to cast their lot with the mercies of mankind and eventual immortality.

Sarah Bernhardt was born in Paris sometime in 1844 to a Jewish mother whose name was Julie Von Hard. Soon after her birth, her father deserted them to take up the practice of law in the French provinces. Julie had no time for her child as she rose to ever greater heights in French society. The mistress of the powerful and wealthy left Sarah to be cared for by a nurse living on a farm in Brittany. Later the nurse married a janitor of a tenement house in the slums of Paris where she, her husband and Sarah lived in a single, smelly room which the sun never penetrated. There the young child was put to work scrubbing the building's floors and performing other menial taks. Her only playground was the filthy alleys of the neighborhood and her first language the obscenities of the streets. Never a healthy child to begin with, she became pale, thin and anemic—to the point where she was dangerously close to contracting tuberculosis at the age of five. The nurse made repeated requests to the mother for money, but Julie refused to answer them.

One day Julie's sister, who also had had a successful career of love affairs, drove up to a neighboring house on "professional business." Sarah was playing in the gutter when she arrived. As she stepped from the carriage, Sarah rushed up to her and with tears in her eyes and pleading in her voice said, "Tante Rosine, take me away! They suffocate me, these walls—always these walls. Take me away, Tante Rosine! I want to see the sky again, and the flowers!" To avoid embarassment, Aunt Rosine led the child indoors and asked the nurse for an explanation, but there was none. Still there was nothing Aunt Rosine could do about it. It was impossible for her to take this child back to her apartment with her lovers. So, to calm her, she said "I will come and take you home tomorrow."

Sarah stood at the window and watched her aunt as she daintily brushed aside her tears with a lace handkerchief and got ready to mount the carriage's steps. Instinctively, she knew her aunt would never be back. Then, just as the carriage was about to move away, Sarah hurled herself from the window onto the pavement below, landing only a few feet away from the carriage. Aunt Rosine screamed and rushed to the broken body of the child which lay motionless. "Oh, you poor child," she cried out as she knelt over the crumpled body. "I shall take you home to your mother." Then, very carefully she gathered the still unconscious but breathing child in her arms and placed her in the carriage. Sarah was to remain an invalid in her mother's home for the next two years. Thus, a five year old was to display all the courage, tenacity and impetuosity in one single moment which would typify her the rest of her turbulent life. It would also enable her to fascinate audiences from the stage even when she was in her seventies and had only one leg. There were to be two other such critical moments in her life.

Anne Sullivan (Macy) was born April 14, 1866 in Feeding Hills, Massachusetts. Her mother became crippled and sick while Anne was still an infant and died before Anne was nine. Her father, a farm day-laborer, spent most of his meager earnings on whiskey. Her brother, Jimmie, was born three years later. He suffered from a tubercular lump on his hip the size of a tea cup.

After their mother died, their father deserted them and they went to live with their father's cousin, John, who was a prosperous tobacco farmer. John and his wife, Statia, had children of their own and Anne Sullivan was such a wilful child even Statia was afraid of her. In fact, one Christmas Anne became so violent when she didn't receive the doll she wanted she broke everything in sight, including her own presents, the others' toys and even the Christmas ornaments. It was then that Statia decided that it was an impossible situation and that she could no longer tolerate Anne's fits of temper. After consulting with the village authorities, it was decided that both children could be declared paupers and, therefore, should be sent to the state infirmary at Tewksbury as wards of the state. Annie was only ten years old at the time.

Soon after they entered the infirmary Jimmie's condition gradually became worse and at his death Annie lost the only friend she had ever had in the world. Tewksbury at that time was a decrepit institution occupied by human derelicts—mild lunatics, epileptics and cripples, along with cockroaches, mice and big, gray rats. Others were afflicted with cancer and venereal diseases and some were dying of tuberculosis. The ward for unwed mothers was especially pitiful. It was more of a place for the dying than the living as the unwanted babies either passed away from neglect or malnutrition. In the summer they were covered with flies and mosquitoes because the windows lacked screens; in the winter they froze from lack of sufficient covers and heat. The State's weekly allowance of $1.75 per patient per week was hardly enough to cover even the most basic of human needs.

The trachoma of the eyes, a virus spread by flies where the most unsanitary conditions exist, which had struck Annie when she was three, now worsened. At first the disease manifested itself with soft, fuzzy lumps inside the eyelids. Unless taken care of by surgery in the early stages, these lumps would become hardened into calluses which, scratching the eyeballs, would eventually result in blindness. Annie's condition was fast approaching this point at Tewksbury despite the fact that they had sent her to Boston for several operations. None had been successful. Thus the weeks, months, and years slipped by. Annie was now fourteen and could recognize the other inmates only by the size and shape of their bodies and by their voices. Her constant hope, nay, obsession, now was to get out of Tewksbury and into a school for the blind.

About this time, the Massachusetts State Board of Charities decided to investigate the incredible stories they were hearing about the place. And, to this end, they appointed a commission headed by F. B. Sanborn, a friend of Ralph Waldo Emerson, to make the investigation. As word of the investigation and the impending visit of the commission reached the institution, Annie became more and more determined to face Mr. Sanborn and tell him her dream. Late one September morning he and several other men arrived and Annie followed them around as they made their inspection, not knowing which one was Mr. Sanborn. Finally, it was late in the day and the men were about to leave. As they approached the gate, Annie felt her dream slipping away. But no, she would not let it. Suddenly, she ran into the middle of the group and shouted "Mr. Sanborn, I want to go to school!" "What's the matter with you, my child?" a voice asked. "I can't see you very well," she replied. "How long have you been here?" But Annie was now so embarrassed by all the attention she had aroused, she couldn't answer. Slowly the group moved away, and Annie ran to her room. That night she cried herself to sleep with disappointment, thinking all hope for leaving Tewksbury was lost.

Several weeks later someone came running up to Annie shouting "Annie, Annie you've got your wish. You're going away to school." It was Maggie Hogan, Annie's one friend in the institution. Maggie had come there as an orphan child with a crippled back and was now a gentle middle-aged woman in charge of Annie's ward and the ward for unwed mothers.

And so it was that one day Anne Sullivan, Helen Keller's savior and great teacher, realized one of the great moments of her life, showing the same tenacity, courage and impulsiveness as Sarah Bernhardt, as she walked out into the sunshine with all her worldly possessions wrapped in a single newspaper. She was escorted by a man from the Board of Charities who was to take her on the train to South Boston where she would enter the most famous school for the blind in the country, The Perkins Institution for the Blind. She was only fourteen years old.

Sarah Bernhardt was now seven and fully recovered from her fall from the window. Her mother decided it was now time for her to go to school. But she proved to be so obstreperous and undisciplined that she had to be taken out and placed in a convent which was called "The Grandchamps Convent of Versailles." The very thought of it terrified young Sarah because it reminded her of a prison she had read about in a book. But it was not to be so. On the first day the Mother Superior of the convent, Mother Ste. Sophie "raised her veil . . . and . . . I then saw the sweetest and merriest face imaginable, with large, child-like blue eyes, a turned-up nose, a laughing mouth with full lips and beautiful, strong, white teeth. She looked so kind, so energetic and so gay that I flung myself at once into her arms."

But neither the Mother Superior nor the quietude of convent life could quell the raging spirits of young Sarah. Three times she was suspended for unruly conduct, before she was finally expelled at 15. Once she feigned a fainting spell at a school ceremony, playing dead so well that the Mother Superior was beside herself with anxiety. Only then did Sarah open her eyes and reveal the whole thing to be a joke. Another time she and six other girls tied bed sheets together and escaped over the convent's walls. Another she was discovered throwing rocks at the King's guard and flirting with a young dragoon. In her spare time she could be found reading forbidden books or eating bonbons. But the last straw, the event which caused her expulsion, was when she climbed the convent wall to flirt with a dragoon in her nightgown. When she had recovered from the cold and fever which beset her following this episode, she was sent home for good.

Thus Sarah Bernhardt ended the period of her formal education at about the same age as Annie Sullivan was commencing hers. For Sarah a tumultuous life in and out or the theater would be her only education for the next ten years. For Annie it would be a rather uneventful eight years of formal schooling for the blind before she would meet her next great challenge in life. But it would be a rocky road. In her first class the teacher asked her to give her name and Annie replied "Annie Sullivan." "Spell it," the teacher said. "I can't spell," Annie replied. "How old are you?" "Fourteen." "Fourteen years old and you can't spell your name," the shocked teacher said. And the whole class laughed.

Later her spelling improved but not to the complete satisfaction of the teacher who mistakenly thought she could shame Annie into doing better. But it only resulted in greater amusement for the class. Finally, Annie could stand it no longer. "Laugh, you silly things," she exploded. "That's all you can do, to the Queen's taste." Annie had used the expression 'to the Queen's taste' without knowing its meaning or how it would reflect on the teacher. The teacher's reaction was immediate, however, as she ordered Annie to leave the room and sit on the stairs outside until the class was over. With this, Annie became furious as she jumped up from her desk, banging it with her hands. Then she ran from the room and slammed the door behind her as she turned and yelled "I will not sit on the stairs! And I will not come back to this class again."

When Mr. Anagnos, the principal, heard about the case, he decided Annie would not only have to return to the class but she would also have to apologize to the teacher or be expelled from the school. But Annie refused. A Miss Mary Moore, Annie's English teacher, knew what this meant—either a return to the deplorable conditions of Tewksbury or a life-time of institutionalization somewhere else. So she interceded with an offer to take Annie in hand as her personal responsibility. This they agreed to and so once a week Miss Moore would take Annie for what was supposed to be a tutoring session in English but actually proved to be much more. When Annie became rude or obstreperous, Miss Moore would merely ignore it and change the subject to something else. In this way Annie failed to get the attention she desired and Miss Moore would correct her grammar and spelling mistakes without chiding her and laughing

at her. Gradually, Annie came to realize her many short-
comings and sought to overcome them. It was Miss
Moore's quiet good manners and tacit assumption that
she and Annie were good friends that finally won Annie
over. The rest of her life Anne Sullivan would consider
Miss Moore the best teacher and the best friend she ever
had.

A brief word about the Perkins Institution for
the Blind. Forty years before Annie entered it, Dr. Samuel Gridley Howe had become world famous as the first
person to teach a blind, deaf and dumb person how to
communicate. The person he taught was one Laura
Bridgman, then a child and now a mature person still at
the institution. The method Dr. Howe devised was the
manual alphabet, the "finger language" by which the
deaf and dumb but not the blind could communicate
with each other. Laura was blind; so he spelled out the
words with his fingers into the palm of her hand and
taught her to spell them back to him. All the children at
Perkins were taught the same method, including Annie,
so that they could communicate with Laura. But most of
them were bored with the method and impatient with
Laura's clumsy handling of idiomatic English. Not Annie. She was fascinated by it, and thus Laura became her
first friend at Perkins.

Every summer the school closed while the children went home to visit with their families. Since Annie
had no home to go to, the teachers arranged for her to do

light housework in a rooming house in Boston. There it was her good luck to meet a young man, a roomer, who took a liking to her and was fascinated by her unusually quick and alert mind. It was he who recommended that a certain Dr. Bradford operate on her failing eyes and the scar tissue which was inexorably blinding her. For days after the operation they kept her eyes bandaged. Finally, when Dr. Bradford ordered the bandages removed, he turned to Annie and said "Open your eyes, Annie." Annie hesitated, terrified to learn the results. "Annie, open your eyes," the doctor insisted. Slowly, hesitantly she squinted, as one would do coming out of a dark cavern into the searing sunlight. Then, with increasing confidence, she opened them even wider. "What can you see?" she heard the doctor say. "I can see you!" Annie cried. "I can see you! I can see your eyes and your nose and your mouth and your hair," she exulted. "I can see!" Annie was then sixteen years old.

Annie was to have another good friend at Perkins, a cultured older lady, the widow of a sea captain, living on Cape Cod, whose daughter had died at about Annie's age. Mrs. Sophia Hopkins had applied for a job at Perkins just to have something to do. Almost immediately Annie and she had become good friends. No two people could have been more unalike—the sedate, prim Mrs. Hopkins with her New England background and gentility and the fiery, impulsive child of immigrant Irish parents. However, both needed each other. Mrs. Hopkins needed to mother someone and someone needed to mother young Annie. By her third year Annie had given up her summer job to spend her summers with Mrs. Hopkins in her comfortable Cape Cod home where they enjoyed each others' friendship and Annie absorbed much of her friend's cultural background. Under those circumstances Annie began to blossom to the extent that by her fourth and fifth years she had become quite a good student. And by the sixth and final year she had excelled to the point where she was chosen as the valedictorian of her class.

Now that she had finished school the question became what would she do with herself. Miss Moore wanted her to go to a normal school and become a teacher. But this took money which Annie didn't have. She thought of becoming a governess for someone's children, but before this could develop, she received a letter at Cape Cod from Mr. Anagnos asking her to read a letter he was enclosing. The letter was from a man in Alabama asking him to recommend a teacher for his six year old daughter who was deaf, blind and dumb. Her name was Helen Keller.

In Paris, the question for Julie Von Hard, Sarah Bernhardt's mother, became what to do with young Sarah since she had been expelled from the convent at fifteen. If the convent and her great liking for the Mother Superior could not contain and satisfy her, could any one or any school? A new "friend", the Duc de Morny, a man of influence and connections, suggested that it was hopeless. But he knew of a Monsieur Auber, the Director of the Conservatory, a school for young actors and actresses. Sarah had shown no particular desire or ability to become an actress, but it was something for her to do and it solved the mother's dilemma for the present. One usually prepared for eighteen months to take the entrance examination, but the sudden decision gave Sarah only nine weeks.

The day she left for the examination, Madam Von Hard turned to her daughter and offered her these words of encouragement "You're too stupid to be much of an actress, but it will keep you out of mischief." Each of the girls before her acted out a scene from a famous play, as it was the custom to do. When it became Sarah's turn, she mounted the stage, turned deathly white and said to the judges, "I shall recite the poem of the two pigeons." "Come now, mademoiselle," snapped one of the judges, "have you not prepared the lines of a play? One acts here; one does not recite fables." "I shall recite the fable of the two pigeons!" Sarah replied defiantly, her eyes flashing. And she did. Whether the judges were more impressed by this display of acting temperament or the influence of the Duc de Morny, it was not known. In any case, Sarah passed the examination and was admitted to the Conservatory.

For the next five years she studied there, distinguishing herself more for the friends she made than her acting ability. Upon graduation, again family, friends and people of influence saw that she was admitted to the most illustrious theater group in Europe, the Comédie Française. A permanent position in this theater meant a lifetime of work and even a pension at the end. She made her debut in "Iphigénie." The next morning a leading French critic, Sarcy, wrote: "Mlle. Bernhardt . . . is a tall, pretty girl with a slender figure and a very pleasing expression; the upper part of her face is remarkably beautiful. She holds herself well, and her enunciation is perfectly clear. This is all that can be said for her at present." After her third appearance at the Comédie in Molière's "Les Femmes Savantes", the same critic wrote: "She was just as insignificant in this as her other two roles. The performance was a very poor affair and gives rise to reflections by no means gay."

When Sarah was nine years old her young cousin dared her to jump a ditch that no one else could jump. In the attempt which failed, her face was bruised and lacerated, her wrist broken and pain racked her whole body. As she was being carried home, someone asked her if she would do it again and her reply was "Yes, I would do it again, quand-même (despite all), if any one dared me again, and I will always do what I want to do all my life." Later she asked her mother for some personal stationery and her mother asked her what motto she wanted printed on it and her reply was "Quand-Même", and she said it in such a furious tone of voice, her aunt was heard to mutter "What a terrible child!"

She would say "quand-même" when she was still acting at 77, even though she had only one leg. And she would say it again one day in October of 1921 when she was struck with one of her many attacks of uremia at 75, with a play to do that night. It was 10 o'clock in the morning when it hit. The doctor was called and found her in a state of shock with a temperature of 93°, her teeth chattering and body shivering under ten blankets and a suffocating room temperature. Along about 4 p.m. she opened her eyes and murmured "All right, I'll leave in an hour." Every one in her family and her doctor pleaded with her to give up the performance for that night, but she hurled aside all their entreaties and demanded that she be dressed. Then, wrapped in furs from head to foot and holding a hot water bottle against her body, she was carried to her car.

When she arrived at the theater, she asked that she be allowed to sleep for an hour, which she did. At 7:30 p.m. she started with her make-up. Her hands shook so much she made three attempts before the task was completed. Then they carried her to the stage and hid her in a cabinet where she would await her initial appearance at the end of the first act. To keep her warm they wrapped her in shawls and surrounded her with electric heaters. When the time came for her appearance, she discarded the shawls, rose, stiffened herself in what appeared to be a superhuman effort and recited her entire speech in a weak but almost normal voice. When it was over, she collapsed back into the cabinet, but it proved only a temporary relapse, as she was able to complete her part in the second and third acts of the play. Afterwards, everyone—actors, stage hands and friends—all wept openly in admiration for the incredible spirit she had shown at her advanced age. The next day she was very weak, but three days later she was completely recovered. No one ever knew how close she had been to death. "Quand-même" was not just a phrase to be stamped and engraved on everything she owned, which she did; it was her very heart and spirit.

Sarah Bernhardt had entered the Comédie Française at 20 expecting to stay for life, but her impetuosity and temper would rule otherwise. "(It was) . . . one of those things, a nothing which change a whole life changed mine," she would say. "My sister, Régina, was the cause . . . involuntarily . . . of the drama which made me leave the Comédie." The incident she referred to occurred at one of those traditional ceremonies of the theater honoring the memory of Molière on his anniversary.

All the members of the Comédie were assembled in the foyer of the theater to salute the bust of the great writer when the signal was given for the start of the ceremony. Every one hurried "to the corridor where the busts were. I was holding my little sister's hand and just in front of us was the very fat and very solemn Mme. Nathalie. She was a 'Sociétaire' of the Comédie, old spiteful and surly." In all the ensuing commotion and confusion little Régina accidently stepped on the train of Nathalie's dress; whereupon Nathalie gave the girl a violent push knocking her against a post holding one of the busts. "Régina screamed out and, as she turned back to me, I saw that her pretty face was bleeding. 'You miserable creature!' I called out to the fat woman and, as she turned around to reply, I slapped her in the face." Pandemonium broke loose, as Nathalie started to faint. It was twenty minutes before everything settled down and the crowd was able to file into the theater.

The next day, after a sleepless night, Sarah received a letter from the theater's manager, M. Thierry, asking her to be at his office at 1 p.m. on a "personal matter." Sarah was there and immediately M. Thierry launched into a "deadly sermon, blamed my want of discipline, absence of respect, and scandalous conduct. 'I have asked her to come,' he added, 'and you must apologize to her before three Sociétaires belonging to the committee. If she consents to forgive you, the committee will consider whether to fine you or to cancel your engagement.' "

For a few minutes Sarah was speechless. But when M. Thierry suggested that he go fetch Mme. Nathalie, she immediately spoke up. "Oh no, do not fetch Mme. Nathalie. I shall not apologize to her. I will leave. I will cancel my engagement at once." With this M.

Thierry became more gentle and polite, asking Sarah to sit down. Then he proceeded to quietly point out all the advantages Sarah would have in staying with the Comédie. At the end of his long discourse, he insisted that he send for Mme. Nathalie. It was then that "I roused up like a wild animal."

"Oh, don't let her come here," I shouted. "I should slap her again." "Well, then, I must ask your mother to come," he said.

"My mother would never come," I replied.

"Then, I will go and call on her."

"It will be quite useless," I persisted. "My mother has given me my liberty, and I am quite free to lead my own life. I alone am responsible for all that I do." And so the conversation ended.

Several days passed, but nothing seemed to have changed at the theater. In fact, one morning Sarah received a request to be present for the reading of a new play. Surprisingly, it was the first time she had ever been asked to such a reading. She was even more astonished when she received the principal role in it. One day, after she had been through five days of rehearsals, she ran into Mme. Nathalie most unexpectedly and unavoidably on the stairway of the Comédie. "I did not know whether to go back downstairs or pass by her . . . my hesitation was noticed by the spiteful woman."

"Oh, you can go by, mademoiselle," Nathalie said. "I have forgiven you, as I have avenged myself. The role you like so much is not to be left to you after all."

Sarah was "thunderstruck" by all this, but chose to make no reply as she proceeded to pass her on the staircase.

All of this occurred on a Tuesday. Friday the rehearsal was cancelled. As she was leaving the theater, the hall porter ran up to her and gave her a letter. It was from the director and it said that her role in the play had been cancelled. At first she was grief-stricken but soon her tears turned into anger as she rushed back into the building and up to the manager's office. There she was told that the manager was not available at that time. "Then, I will wait," Sarah replied. Fifteen minutes passed, then a half hour, then an hour and Sarah could stand it no longer. She jumped up from her chair, rushed by the office boy and secretary who tried to restrain her, and plunged into Monsieur Thierry's office. There she let forth such a stream of eloquence and fury, interrupted by occasional great sobs, that M. Thierry just "gazed at me in bewilderment." Finally, when all her energy had been spent, she collapsed in an armchair with exhaustion. "I will leave at once," she sighed. "Give me back my engagement and I will send you back mine."

M. Thierry thought for a minute, obviously tired of all the argumentation and emotional strain involved. Then, he called in his secretary and told him to get Sarah's engagement. In a few minutes the secretary returned with the paper and M. Thierry handed it to Sarah, saying "Here is your mother's signature, mademoiselle. I leave you free to bring it back to me within forty-eight hours. If I don't receive it I shall consider that you are no longer a member of the theater. But, believe me, you are acting unwisely."

Sarah did not answer him. That night she sent back her copy of the engagement bearing M. Thierry's signature and she tore up the one her mother had signed.

If Sarah Bernhardt's first great crisis and moment—when she threw herself out the window at age five—saved her from a life in the slums; her second—the slapping of Mme. Nathalie—appeared to end a most promising acting career with the most prestigious theatrical group in Europe. She was twenty years old.

"As for me, I am not placid," she would say. "I am active, and always ready for a fight, and what I want I always want immediately." Once when she was in the same compartment of a train with a German Army officer and he refused to either stop smoking his pipe or open the window at Sarah's request, Sarah solved the problem quite easily. She just smashed in the window with her elbow.

It would be twelve tumultuous years before she would return to the Comédie Française, but then they would want her badly.

Anne Sullivan would arrive on the spacious grounds of Captain Arthur Keller's estate in Tuscumbia, Alabama on March 5, 1887, only a month from her twenty-first birthday. Captain Keller was a confederate veteran, newspaper editor, gentleman farmer and leading citi-

zen of the community. Had Mr. Anagnos told him anything of Anne Sullivan's background, her limited
schooling of six years, no real training or experience in
the teaching of the deaf and blind, he and Mrs. Keller
never would have hired her. In fact, they would have
been horrified if they had known of her childhood background and Tewksbury. And Anne herself probably
would not have taken the position had she known that
the six year old Helen Keller was a wild, undisciplined
animal who had almost killed her younger sister when
she dumped her out of her cradle.

Captain and Mrs. Keller in their compassion
had made no effort whatsoever to discipline their unfor-
tunate daughter. The result was that whenever Helen
couldn't get her way, she had a tantrum. Rather than
fight her, days on end would pass when they would allow her to go unwashed and uncombed. Helen was a
strong child and she tyrannized the entire household
with her tantrums and sheer physical strength. In fact,
her strength was such that within the first two days of
Anne's arrival she had knocked out two of her front
teeth. After they had had a few more of these encoun-
ters, Anne concluded there was nothing she could do for
Helen unless she could gain control over her. She only
hoped that in doing so she would not break the child's
spirit.

The battleground for the test developed quite
unexpectedly one morning at the breakfast table. Until

now no one had ever tried to teach Helen how to sit down at the table and eat like other people. It was her habit to wander about the table taking whatever she wanted from anyone's plate, while her parents ignored her. This morning, however, Annie had decided that she would not let her take anything from her plate. Every time she tried, Anne would slap her hand. Finally, Helen became so frustrated she threw herself on the floor kicking and screaming in a tantrum. It took all the strength Anne could muster to corral the child and put her in a chair by the table. Then she forced a spoon in her hand and, taking hold of it, tried to make her feed herself. But Helen would have none of it. Each time she would throw the spoon on the floor and Anne would then drag the child from the chair, take her to the spoon and try to make her pick it up. Then she would put her back in the chair and the whole process would begin over again.

Meanwhile, Captain and Mrs. Keller, horrified by the scene, had left the room, and Annie had locked the door behind them. She sat down to try to finish her breakfast, but Helen crept behind her and tried to pull the chair out from her. When that didn't succeed, she would pinch Annie and each time Annie would slap her hand. This too was repeated several times. In all the scuffling and attention she was getting from Annie, Helen was not aware that her parents had left the room until she walked around the table and discovered they were not in their customary seats. Now, feeling very alone and somewhat contrite, she returned to Annie and with a puzzled look raised her hand to her mouth signifying she wanted to eat. Then she climbed back on her chair and submissively let Annie help her finish her breakfast.

But the battle was not over. As soon as she had finished her breakfast, she tore the napkin from her neck, threw it on the floor and rushed to the door, only to find it locked. Again all the fury in her little body broke loose as she kicked and pounded at the door screaming and howling. Annie grabbed her and, using all the strength she had, forced her back to the table where she made her pick up her napkin. She tried to show her how it should be folded, but Helen would take it in her hands, throw it on the floor and then fall upon it. And Annie would make her pick it up and try again to show her how to fold it, only to have Helen toss it on the floor again and again. Finally, emotionally and physically exhausted, Annie decided to leave her alone. Soon the wailing and screaming became less and less, and quiet little sobs took their place, as Helen sat dutifully in her chair and let Annie show her how to fold a napkin. It was now approaching the noon hour as Annie let a thoroughly subdued and chastened child out of the room and into the garden to play. Annie, spent and exhausted, went upstairs to her room and cried herself to sleep.

A couple of days later Helen again started to

misbehave at the table and Annie was about to take her out of the room when Captain Keller ordered her back.

"No child of mine," he stormed, "is ever going to be sent away from the table hungry!" And Mrs. Keller added "I know we shouldn't interfere, but we feel so sorry for her."

"Yes, but she's got to learn to obey me before I can help her," Annie replied. "I can't do anything with her the way she is."

From the beginning Captain Keller had been the more difficult to deal with whereas Mrs. Keller was more sympathetic to Anne's purposes. Repeatedly Annie had suggested that she could do a lot more with her if she could just have her alone for awhile. But Captain Keller would hear none of this. In fact, several times he even threatened to send "that Yankee girl" home. But the Kellers knew that Annie was their last and only hope and if Annie didn't succeed in controlling her, she would end up in a home for the feeble-minded or in a strait jacket.

Finally the two women convinced him that it would be best for everyone if Annie and Helen moved into a cottage on the Keller grounds to live by themselves. And so the desperation of two parents and the determination of an outsider served each other in a crisis which saved the life and brilliant mind of Helen Keller. The moment—the breakfast table incident—was as much Annie's as it was Helen's so intertwined did their lives become, but probably neither one realized it at the time. Within a month they would, when Annie taught her her first word in the manual alphabet, "Water". It's an oft-told story which bears repeating, but first let us hear what Anne Sullivan has to say about herself.

In the first place she never regarded herself as an educator despite the fact that Albert Einstein once said her work "has in it an element of the superhuman." She never recorded in a book her theories on education for the guidance of other teachers. Nor did she ever feel that she had any burning message to convey to others. "If I had felt so, I would have left Helen long ago to preach it," she would say. Yet she would have this trenchant insight into her early relationship with Helen Keller: "She refused to be caressed and there was no way of appealing to her affection or childish love of approbation . . . thus, it is, we study, plan, and prepare ourselves for a task and when the hour for action arrives, we find that the system . . . does not fit the occasion; and then there is nothing for us to do but rely on something within us, some innate capacity for knowing and doing, which we did not know we possessed until the hour of our great need brought it to light." If anything, it might have been the harsh, cruel world of Tewksbury and her own eye affliction which prepared her best for her task. The first put steel in her back; the second, the sympathy and understanding to deal with the problem. Her own determination and boundless spirit were God-given and revealed themselves in her childhood struggles.

But the technique—the manual alphabet—she had learned at Perkins. And this she started using on Helen immediately after her arrival at the Kellers. At first it was just an entertaining game and the words she spelled out on the palm of Helen's hand meant nothing to her. In fact, they had become repetitious and boring. But Annie persisted as she continued to fight Helen's tantrums, confident that if Laura Bridgman could learn it, Helen—who she thought was a brighter child—could too. The only difference was that Laura had been a placid, docile child who gave no one any trouble as she sought to learn.

Now it was a warm spring day—April 5, 1887 to be exact (one month and two days after Annie's arrival) —and Helen and Annie were resting in the vine-covered pump house located in the Keller backyard. They were not exactly resting because Annie was trying desperately to teach Helen the difference between a cup and water by the manual alphabet. Helen held a cup in one hand as Annie poured water in it, letting it overflow on Helen's hand as she spelled out C-U-P or W-A-T-E-R in the other hand. But try as she might, Helen could not distinguish between the two words. Increasingly her frustration mounted until at one point she became so infuriated she smashed her favorite doll against the hard bricks. C-U-P just meant nothing to her and neither did W-A-T-E-R. So Annie decided to concentrate on one word— W-A-T-E-R. Over and over again she would let the cool water spill over the cup and into Helen's hand and on her wrist as she spelled out W-A-T-E-R, W-A-T-E-R, W-A-T-E-R in the other hand.

Suddenly Helen's little body stiffened and it appeared as if she had stopped breathing. Then, as one transfixed, she groped and stumbled her way, reaching for Annie's hand. When she found it, she grasped it and with trembling fingers started to spell out W-A-T..on the palm. Annie gave her an ecouraging pat on the shoulder. With great delight Helen finished the spelling. Annie would never forget the expression on Helen's face at that moment. She knew the breakthrough had come. Then frantically Helen groped for the pump, the trellis, even the ground as she touched each and then ran to Annie to have her spell it out in her hand. A whole new world had opened up. Each thing had a name! No longer were they just people, physical bodies; it was Mama, it was Papa—to their great delight. The baby was sister and Annie was Teacher, as she would be called the rest of her life during their constant companionship. Tears streamed down Annie's cheeks as the two slowly made their way back to the house touching and spelling everything within reach. By evening Helen had learned thirty new words, and a sleepy, contented little girl for the first time snuggled up to her teacher and kissed her goodnight. Annie's heart was full of thanksgiving. Never again would she feel that bottomless emptiness she felt when Jimmie died. Impetuosity may have freed the nine year old Anne Sullivan from being institutionalized for life at Tewksbury, but it was her good instincts plus intelligence and determination which gave her life at twenty-one meaning and also saved the life of her brilliant pupil.

In later years, Dr. Alexander Graham Bell, whose interest in the deaf because of his own affliction was well-known, asked Anne Sullivan what method she used. "M-m-method," replied Annie, "I—well—I don't really have any method. I just keep trying new things as I think of them. Some of them work. Some don't."

On October 19, 1936, Anne Sullivan Macy (she was married briefly) died quietly at the age of 70, her life long overshadowed by the accomplishments of her famous pupil. She was the "Easter morning of my life," Helen Keller would say as her body was cremated and laid to rest next to Woodrow Wilson's in the National Cathedral in Washington, D.C.

After her graduation from Radcliffe College cum laude, Helen Keller became world-renowned as a lecturer and writer. She lived to be 88, but she never forgot Anne Sullivan. "I feel her being is inseparable from my own and that the footsteps of my life are hers. There is not a talent, or an inspiration or a joy in me that has not been awakened by her loving touch." She too was laid to rest next to her life-long companion in the National Cathedral.

Sarah Bernhardt's greatest and most ennobling

moment probably never occurred in the theater but rather in an impulsive act of self-sacrifice during the most serious love affair of her life—an act which forever cast her lot and destiny with a life in the theater.

Following her expulsion from the Comédie Française and a sojourn in Spain, she returned to Paris and gained employment with a theatrical group called the Gymnase. Once when they were called upon to entertain before the King of France, Napoleon III, Sarah, who had always been a great admirer of Victor Hugo, unwittingly chose to recite the verse of this well-known critic of French royalty. In the midst of her performance, the stunned king and his entourage abruptly rose and left the room leaving Sarah all alone. Immediately the director of the group appeared from the wings of the stage hurling insult after insult at the embarrassed Bernhardt and grabbing her wrist so hard she cried out in pain. Suddenly from the far end of the room she heard a man's voice saying "Kindly leave that child alone." "Why don't you mind your own business, sir," the director replied. "But who are you anyway?" "I am the Prince Henri de Ligne," the voice answered, "and I will not allow a woman to be insulted in my presence, especially a young woman who is pretty, naive and defenseless, like this young lady." The director quietly left the stage, leaving Sarah and her unknown defender alone.

Thus began a romance which lasted uninterruptedly throughout 1864 until one day the Prince was ordered by the Belgian government to perform several missions outside the country. Sarah was now pregnant, but she refused to let the Prince know for fear he would come back to her not for her own sake but for the sake of the child. On December 22, 1865 Maurice Bernhardt was born out of wedlock, the father unknown. Sarah was then only twenty years and two months old. Eventually Prince Henri returned and their romance continued and their love for each other grew stronger than ever. Finally, he came to the realization that their love was of such magnitude that, despite his title, the overwhelming op-postion of his family to a marriage to a woman of Jewish descent and a commoner, he proposed marriage to her. Sarah was ecstatic. There was only one condition, he said. She must give up her career in the theater. Sarah agreed to this with surprising alacrity. After all, she thought, she was not making any great sacrifice since up to now she had enjoyed very little success in the theater and there was very little prospect for any in the future.

However, her moment of happiness was all too fleeting. One day there was a knock on her door and a man entered who introduced himself as Prince Henri's uncle, General de Ligne. He explained that the Prince's father had become ill so the family had asked him to carry their message to her. It was in the form of an ultimatum. If she persisted in the marriage, she should know that his parents would then strip their son of all his family's privileges and future patrimony. Did she have any right to inflict this fate upon the man she loved? Stunned and shocked by this harsh turn of events, Sarah said nothing.

Sarah slept very little that night, tormented and torn between her love for Prince Henri and the harm they said she would inflict upon him. But she had reached a decision. She could not seek the help of the Duc de Morny, her mother's "friend" and man of influence, who had helped her so much in the past. He was now dead. So she sought out the kind-hearted Director of the Beaux Arts, Camille Doucet, and said "It doesn't matter how . . . or on what terms . . . but I must get an engagement immediately in some play . . . not just one play but for a long contract . . . something with important penalties so that in no case can I recover my freedom." Having said this, she explained to him the reason behind it. Doucet was touched by the story and said that he would talk to the management of the Odéon Theater, over which he had a great deal of influence. Two days later Sarah received a visit from one Félix Duquesne from the Odéon Theater. He had with him a three year contract already signed by him and the management. "Read this," he said, "and if the terms are suitable, sign it and return it to us and you will make your debut at the Odéon in a fortnight."

Ironically, as Duquesne was leaving Prince Henri arrived, and he immediately demanded an explanation for the stranger's appearance. Sarah explained that he had come with an offer of a contract and she showed it to him, saying that she was convinced their marriage would not work and this was a great opportunity for her. At first Prince Henri thought Sarah was teasing and it was all a bad joke—until she picked up the contract and proceeded to sign it. The Prince was infuriated, pacing back and forth in the room and in great agitation accused his love of the "utmost duplicity." "Evidently those who wish to separate me from you were right. A cheap actress never changes! She always remains what she is and lives only for one passion, the stage."

Sarah bit her lip and fought back the tears but said nothing about General de Ligne's visit, although her heart cried out to say: "It isn't true! I adore you! And it is only out of love for you that I made this decision." She knew that if she told the truth, it would only strengthen his resolve to marry her at the risk of a break with his family. Finally when all arguments had been exhausted and the Prince had gone—forever—Sarah collapsed on the floor and a violent fever seized her frail body. For one month it was not known whether she would live or die. It was not until December 1866—one year after the birth of her son—that Sarah had recovered enough to make her debut with the Odéon, the second most prominent theater in France. Again it attracted little attention. Sarah Bernhardt had only one other love affair in her lifetime and it was brief and disastrous. He was a charmer of all the ladies, but a known morphine addict, known to everyone but Sarah. They were married for seven years—until his death in his late forties—but they lived together only for the first year of their married life and had no children.

Perhaps it was impulsive, even reckless that Sarah Bernhardt sacrificed herself for the future of the only man she ever really loved, Prince Henri. But it was also the greatest and most decisive moment in her life because, perhaps unknowingly, she had opted for a life in the theater, a life which would last uninterruptedly for the next 56 years. There was now no man, no affair which could take the place of this love.

Sarah Bernhardt estimated her life-time earnings at $9 million and, distrusting banks, she insisted that all of it be paid in gold at the end of each performance. Yet she died penniless, and at the end was living off the sale of her jewelry. Much of her earnings went to the support of her friends and relatives. She paid generous wages but was irregular in her payments, as she was always in debt. Some of her servants were of long standing; others, such as her cook and kitchenmaid, she changed twice a month. As always, she acted on impulse and if she wanted a letter delivered immediately, she would dispatch her secretary anywhere in France to have it delivered in person. She would drive a hard bargain for her salary; then spend money recklessly on shopping orgies or on her elaborate summer home at Belle Isle off the coast of Brittany, which consisted of several villas for her family and friends, tennis courts and boats, in which she had invested well over four million francs.

Early in life the doctors had told her that her frail body could not long stand the rigors of fourteen and fifteen hour days. Some would say it was an act of defiance that she had a rosewood coffin built and erected in her home; her critics would say it was just a publicity stunt, especially when she let photographers take her picture in it and when she cluttered her house with a menagerie of dogs, cats and even lion cubs. Some said her house was more of a museum than a home. She dressed in colorful, swirling silks and velvets trimmed with fur and she thought everyone should dress this way, even children— else how would anyone know who they belonged to, if they dressed too simply. She painted, sculptured and wrote, all with a degree of competence. But she said music was only noise to her, that she was tone-deaf. Yet she had developed a weak voice into one of her greatest attributes, as was her phenomenal memory. She never really conquered stage fright and her hands were cold before every performance, especially if she expected a friendly audience. If she thought it was going to be hostile, she was calm and collected, poised and ready to conquer it.

Although she said she was shy and afraid of everything, her wild outbursts of temper continued into adulthood. But there was nothing crafty or cunning in her nature nor in her self-portrait: "From the profile, I look like a goat—full-faced like a lioness." She was kind. Once she stayed all night with an injured stage hand, though there were others to care for him. When asked why she did it, she replied "I shall be sure (he's alright) if I stay here. If I go home, I shall not." Another time a silly girl became so infatuated with "L'Aiglon" that she refused all suitors and drove her parents to despair. "Send her to me," Sarah said. Sarah greeted the girl in her dressing room without make-up and in a tattered dressing gown. "This is what I really look like," she told her. "There is no such person as 'L'Aiglon' except on the stage." Later the young girl married and became a mother, and Sarah Bernhardt added still another baby to her long list of godchildren.

In 1905 (October) while acting in Rio de Janeiro, she first injured her leg. Phlebitis set in and by 1911 she could not take a step without leaning on someone's arm. And by 1913 it was necessary to arrange the furniture on the set so that she didn't have to take more than two steps at a time. Her right leg was removed February 23, 1915. Yet in 1916 she was carried in a wheel chair to the front to entertain the soldiers. In the winter of 1916–17 she made the last of her many tours of the United States. As her life was expiring in 1923 she contracted to make a motion picture with an American producer. However, she was too ill to leave the house. When she could no longer be filmed in the sitting room, she said, "Film me in bed!" Quand-même!

On March 21, 1923 she had her fifth attack of uremia. On March 25, she went into a coma and one day later she died without regaining consciousness. She was 79 years old.

V

DETERMINATION

LENIN

"We must not wait. We may lose everything."

LENIN

T HERE WAS "nothing to document the formula of
mother or father fixation, no unhappy family life, malad-
justed childhood, youthful rebellion against domestic
tyranny, no traces of a sense of inferiority due to failure
at school or in childhood competitive sports, no sign of
queerness or abnormality."

In short, there was nothing in the childhood or
family life, no psychological ambiance whatsoever, to
nurture a rebellion in the greatest revolutionist of our
time or perhaps of any time, for that matter. Vladimar
Ilyich Ulyanov (Lenin) was born April 22, 1870, one of
six children of Ilya Nikolaevich and Maria Alexandrovna
Ulyanov in the province of Simbirsk, Russia. His father
was a man of modest means but a respected citizen in the
bureaucratic and intellectual life of the community, first
as a provincial school inspector, then as Superintendent
of Schools, a position which was regarded as one of the
minor nobility.

The family was closely knit and Lenin's childhood and adolescent years were believed to be almost

idyllically happy. The family "knew neither want nor rebellion . . . the household was one breathing order, peace, conscientious devotion to duty, domestic simplicity and quiet affection." As a child, Lenin had "a healthy body, a lively brain, an ironical sense of fun, and an ability to excell easily in studies, sports and tests of strength." In fact, the children could not recall witnessing a quarrel or disagreement between their parents, at least in their presence.

Lenin's grandfather had died when his father, Ilya, was only seven years old, and so Ilya's brother, who was thirteen years his senior, stopped his own schooling to support the family. Thus began the long climb upwards from being a family of plebians to that of the nobility in the only way possible at that time—by service to the state. When Ilya was finally appointed Director of the Primary Schools for the whole province, after years as a teacher of physics and mathematics, the office carried with it the title of "state councillor". This was an hereditary title which meant that when Lenin was three years old he would become a nobleman and his father would now be addressed as "Your Excellency". Someday Lenin would be too. The position corresponded roughly to that of a major general in the army.

Lenin's mother, Maria Alexandrovna Ulyanova, was four years younger than her husband and would outlive him by thirty years. He died in January 1886 of a family affliction, arteriosclerosis, which had shortened

the life of his father and would also take the life of his son
prematurely. Maria's most outstanding trait was her devotion to her family. From the time of her husband's
death when Lenin was 16 until her own at 81 in 1916,
one year before her son became head of the new Russian
State, she was tireless in serving the needs of her family.
Even though she would see all of her children arrested at
one time or another, she never once wavered in her devotion or failed to humiliate herself in pleading their
cases before official Russia. Even under reduced financial
circumstances, she would labor lovingly and faithfully to
their needs, whether in exile or imprisonment, sending
them money, clothes, books and food. Often she would
move to be closer to them. And not once did she castigate
them for their misdeeds or waiver "in her loyalty however much official society branded them criminals or
monsters." Freud once said that any one who was the
"indisputable favorite of his mother would keep for life
the feeling of a conqueror, that confidence of success that
often induces real success." Lenin was such a person.

     He would need all the confidence he could
muster when, one year after his father's death, his older
brother, Alexander, and four co-conspirators were executed for plotting against the Tsar. And he would need it
for the next 35 years of his short life when time after time
he would stand alone as a majority of one against his fellow Bolshevicks, hopelessly defeated, deserted, even
thought to be insane, only to rise up again. Later that

year he would enter Kazan University, but after only
three months, on December 4, 1887, he was arrested
and expelled for sitting quietly in the front row of the
school assembly hall while a few of his fellow conspira-
tors drew up a list of demands for their rights.

Despite his mother's urgent pleadings to the
Minister of Education, he was not allowed to re-enter the
university. They said, however, he would be permitted
to take the exams for the four-year course in jurispru-
dence in the spring and fall of 1891. Lenin once said that
the only way he learned to master English, French and
German was "to break the backbone of the language at
the outset" by learning all the verbs, adverbs and adjec-
tives, rules of grammar and syntax. This he was to do not
only in preparing for the examinations in law and the
study of Karl Marx at this time, but later he would apply
it to the chaos that was Russia after he assumed power.
Thus he would become known as the master of organizational detail. He took only a little over one year to prepare for the law exams, and then he passed them with the
highest possible grades and on November 27, 1891 was
awarded his diploma with honors. He stood first in his
class on the exams. For the next year and a half he served
as a junior attorney in a law firm in Samara where he
handled ten cases of petty theft and failed to get an ac-
quittal verdict in any one of them.

Thus for six years (1887–1893) Lenin had studied, questioned, examined and soaked up knowledge like

a sponge. Now, at 23, already bald except at the temples
and a small reddish beard, his face was worn and his skin
was a parched yellow-brown. He was already known as
an "old man". It was during this period that he became a
confirmed, professional revolutionary. In conversation
about art or literature, he was unimpressive and unin-
spired. But when the subject matter turned to politics, he
became a changed man—thoroughly aroused and reveal-
ing a mind of great brilliance and power. His every re-
mark showed deep reflection and study despite the fact
his life up to now had been quite unsophisticated. He
spoke with a machine-like rapidity in a rather high-
pitched voice that overwhelmed his listeners with its
knowledge and force.

In 1893 he moved to St. Petersburg (later Petrograd, then Leningrad) and there with the aid of fellow
Communists made plans for the publication of a paper to
be called "The Workers' Cause". But before it could be
published he was arrested in December 1895 and sentenced to one year in prison and three years of exile in
eastern Siberia. Since he was a political prisoner and not
charged with acts of terrorism, his sentence did not in-
clude hard labor and he was permitted to receive all the
food, books and writing materials he wanted while in
prison. In fact, he once said jokingly that he was entertaining the idea of opening a prison store. Unlike the Stalin days, the food was adequate and the isolation conducive to studying and writing. It was during this period

that he wrote and made plans to publish the major theo-
retical work of his lifetime, "The Development of Capi-
talism in Russia", which was published without inter-
ference from the state's censor during his last year in Siberia in 1899. His greatest worry on being sent to Siberia
was not the physical punishment but rather the un-
founded fear that the materials for his research would not
be available there.

      Upon being released from the House of Prelim-
inary Detention, he was allowed one week in St. Petersburg to say his farewells and to make arrangements on
his own time and at his own expense for the trip to Shushenskoye, Siberia, his place of exile. He arrived there
on May 20, 1896. With an allowance of 8 rubles per
month ($4.00) he was able to rent a furnished room in a
peasant's cottage, pay for his food and have his laundry
and mending done. It was not exactly a luxurious life,
but it was tolerable. Prisoners were even allowed to seek
outside work and visit each other between neighboring
villages. Some brought their wives or mothers there to
keep house for them.

      There were three weddings performed while
Lenin was there, including that of his own to Nadezhda
Krupskaya in 1898. Nadezhda herself had been arrested
and sentenced to exile. She had requested that she and
her mother be sent to Shushenskoye and her request had
been granted. Under these circumstances, Lenin grew
plump and even forgot the name of the mineral water he

drank for his stomach trouble. Although other Marxists in exile suffered tuberculosis, contracted typhus, went mad or had nervous break-downs trying to support large families, Lenin's life was relatively serene. He even became the champion chess player in the area and Nadezhda proved to be an ideal comrade and secretary who "subordinated herself completely to his work."

From his release in 1899 until his premature death in 1924, Lenin's life would be one of constant turmoil and confrontation not so much with the established authorities as with his fellow Marxists. Sometimes the acrimony became so bitter, Lenin was deserted by all but his closest associates and even they could become "traitors" to him if they did not follow his policy. Standing alone without any apparent support, it was he who professed to speak for the Bolshevick (after Bolshinstvo, meaning majority) professional revolutionaries when, in fact, they were not. More often the social democrats or doctrinaire theoreticians, the willing compromisers, called Menshevicks (after Menshinstvo, meaning minority) were in the majority. But you were either for Lenin and his theory of the dictatorship of the proletariat or you were against him—there was no middle ground. Being a very disciplined person, he demanded the same kind of discipline in others in absolute terms. He neither smoked nor drank.

Once in later years during the recital of Beethoven's "Appassionata" he turned to his friend Maxim Gorky and said "It is marvelous superhuman music . . . what marvelous things human beings can do . . . but I can't listen to music too often . . . it makes me want to say kind, stupid things and pat the heads of people . . . but now one must not pat any one's head—they might bite off your hand, and you have to beat them on the head, beat them without mercy." By then he had sold his body and soul to the dictates and cruelties of the revolution.

Soon after he returned from Siberia, he took up residence in Munich and, with a small group of Communists, published the first issue of Iskra (The Spark) on December 21, 1900 in Leipzig, Germany, for underground distribution to Russia. When one Struve, a member of the editorial staff, deserted Marxism and went over to the liberals, Lenin denounced him in an editorial and called him a traitor. When a friend asked Lenin how he could do this to Struve and that it might prompt some one to kill him, Lenin replied coldly, "He deserves to die."

While serious dissension was developing on the Iskra, the first party Congress was being held in Brussels in the summer of 1903. After two and one-half years of careful planning they could find only 60 revolutionaries who would attend and only four of these were workingmen, the rest being intellectuals. As the small group moved surreptitiously from one union hall to the other to avoid detection, nothing but discord and bitterness developed. Although Lenin dominated the Congress, the chairman, Plekhanov, could muster only 22 out of a possible 44 votes, the rest being abstentions, in his bid to retain the chairmanship. Such was the "majority" (bolshinstvo) out of which the Bolshevick Communist party was born.

Within six months Plekhanov had switched to the side of the Social Democrats, which left Lenin with a minority on the editorial board of Iskra. Lenin himself resigned the editorship rather than share its authority with the Social Democrats amid such epithets as "despot and terrorist" which were flung at him by Trotsky. Others would call him "autocrat", "copperhead", "obstinate" and "narrow-minded". Even Trotsky would say Lenin meant "dictatorship OVER the proletariat" when he used the phrase "dictatorship OF the proletariat".

A few months later Lenin's hand-picked Central Committee and Party Council turned against him. Yet he still claimed he spoke for the majority of the Party and summoned the Central Committee to wage a fight to the finish. Instead the Committee answered with a vote of censure and asked that negotiations be started to make peace with the Mensheviks. Approaching a nervous breakdown, Lenin resigned from all committees and he and Krupskaya shouldered their knapsacks and went tramping through the mountains of Switzerland for a month.

Returning refreshed from Switzerland, he immediately set to work starting a new newspaper. By

Christmas 1904 he had succeeded in founding the "Vpered" (Forward) and had recruited 22 new members to the Bolshevik Party. Many of these would later become members of the general staff, thus enabling Lenin to regain control over the Central Committee. Despite his power, however, the London Congress of 1907 voted against him and in favor of dissolving all fighting units, strong-arm squads and armed robberies which had been fostered by the Party. Lenin refused to accept this decision of the Congress and so the raids continued inside Russia, even though Lenin himself had given up all hope for an armed uprising by mid-1907. It was "one man against a whole Party" they said at the Congress of Socialist International in Copenhagen in the summer of 1910. When some one asked one of his opponents how Lenin could ruin a whole Party, his reply was "because there is no other man who thinks and dreams nothing but revolution twenty-four hours a day."

While Lenin was living in the security of foreign capitals and preaching revolution in sidewalk cafés, the countryside of Russia, especially between 1901 and 1903, had become a seething cauldron of revolutionary activity. The communists were not alone in their political activities. There was the Social Revolutionary Party trying to organize the peasantry and the Constitutional Democratic Party proselytizing the liberal intelligentsia. Meanwhile, the peasants had taken the law into their own hands and were harvesting forbidden hay and cutting forbidden timber belonging to their masters. Any owner who resisted might find himself either murdered or his manor house burned to the ground.

Although there was no organized labor movement (unions were not legalized until 1906), strikes became ever more frequent. And excitable workingmen jammed the urban squares hurling epithets and rocks at the police while students rioted and murdered high governmental officials including the Minister of Education. In effect, the established order was crumbling: Count Leo Tolstoy was excommunicated by the Church; two Princes from the House of Trubetskoi and two from the House of Dolgoruki declared their support of the liberals; Prince Obolenski became a contributor to the underground revolutionary organ, Iskra, founded by Lenin, and even an organizer of a new liberal party, The Constitutional Democratic Party. Even millionaire industrialists like Morozov gave heavily to the underground. From 1904 until his death by suicide in 1905, he gave $1,000 per month through his employee, engineer Krassin, who noted in his memoirs that many bank directors and state officials contributed secretly but liberally to the revolutionary forces.

The eminent historian, J. H. Plumb, has noted that history is full of surprises such as the abolition of slavery and the decline in rate of population growth just when it is least expected—and it was one of Lenin's "most inspired" insights that he recognized this ability of history to create surprises. The best an historian can do, Plumb would say, is to teach others to be wary of this, especially in periods of rampant inflation which "dislocates belief and rots social structures and institutions." Thus, despite Karl Marx's theory that the most fertile seed bed for class struggle and a revolution existed in an urban, highly industrialized society, Lenin recognized that Russia with its basic rural, peasant economy was ripe for revolution in the early twentieth century.

To the casual observer, this would not appear to be so at all. Russia, like the rest of Europe, had a growing, expanding economy. Industrial production was on the upswing, in fact growing by leaps and bounds. In the period 1890–1899, pig iron production increased 108% as compared to England's 18% and the United States' 50%; coal production grew 131% compared to England's 22% and the U.S.'s 61%; and iron and steel production 116% to England's 80% and the U.S.'s 63%. Her cotton industry was second only to England and the United States. By 1900, Russia may not have had the largest industrial working class in Europe, but it was one of the most concentrated. For instance, 14% of the factories in Germany had a work force of more than 500 men; in Russia there were 34%. And while Germany had only 8% employed in factories with more than 1,000 employees, Russia had 24%.

Meanwhile, Piotr Arkadevich Stolypin, Premier of Russia from 1906–1911, sought to fight the revo-

lutionary movement with a two-edged sword, severe re-
pression and sweeping land reforms. Between 1907–1914
over two million peasant families became individual pro-
prietors of small strips of land. And by January 1916 six
million of the sixteen million eligible families had made
application for individual ownership. Lenin often said
that his revolution was a race against Stolypin's reforms
and he admitted that, because of them, he didn't expect
to live to see the revolution.

However, two unforeseen but catastrophic
events were to take place to bring the revolution closer at
hand. One was the devasting effect of Russia's participa-
tion in World War I and the reverses it suffered at the
hands of the Germans and Austrians. The other was the
rise to power of the weakling Tsar Nicholas II (1894-
1917) whose marriage to the German Princess Alix of
Hesse, the Empress Alexandra Feodorovna, produced in
1904 their only son and heir, Tsarevich Alexis, a hemo-
philiac. Unaccountably, Alexis' bleeding could be
checked only by the diabolical religious fervor of one
man, the semi-illiterate peasant monk, Grigori Rasputin,
who thus gained a powerful hold over the Empress and
in turn the Tsar. He had no political program whatsoever other than to promote unscrupulous and reaction-
ary bureaucrats and friends to high positions in government, which led to further undermining of the aristoc-
racy.

The greatest general strike in the history of

Russia, or any country, occurred in 1905, closing down
the railroads, telegraph facilities, steel, textile, metallur-
gical factories and plants of all kinds. But Lenin who was
living in Geneva at the time was not able to participate in
it because the agent who was to meet him in Stockholm
with a forged passport never showed up. The strike
forced from the Tsar a pledge of civil liberties including
freedom of speech and press, the promise of a Constitution and a parliament, which later became known as the
Duma, and amnesty for all political prisoners. At this
point, Trotsky had become the outstanding leader of the
Soviet apparatus and for once the Bolsheviks and Mensheviks cooperated with each other, each accepting the
revolutionary concepts of the general strike, the armed
uprising and the dictatorship of the proletariat. In fact,
the demand for unity was so great neither side dared op-
pose it.

  During all this Lenin maintained an outward
pose of being conciliatory. But he was careful to keep his
factional apparatus together such as it was while the
Mensheviks permitted theirs to disintegrate. By 1909
Krupskaya, his wife, would write, "we have no people at
all." Spies and apathy had ruined the Party in Russia and
Lenin's followers abroad would either desert him or be
read out of the faction by him. The "Party" to Lenin was
any two or three people who would follow his dictates.
As Bolshevik bands degenerated into banditry and its underground became riddled with spies from the state, stu-

dents turned away from politics to the tavern and brothel and workingmen rode a wave of drunkenness and gambling while Rasputin continued to corrupt the Court and the authority of the state. Artsybashev's popular "Sanin", published in 1907, typified the times—a story of suicides, seductions, glorification of the body, physical joys and denigration of all moral principles and values. "Among the young eroticism and suicide became mass phenomena with the same headlong extremism that had been given the revolution."

In May 1912 Lenin and the Bolsheviks started a new daily newspaper, Pravda, which was published in St. Petersburg (now Leningrad). Lenin wrote most of the editorials and Roman Malinovsky, Lenin's deputy inside Russia and the organizational leader there, became its publisher. He also sat in the fourth Imperial Duma as leader of the Bolshevik faction of five deputies (there were seven Menshevik deputies in the same Duma). Many times Lenin was warned that Malinovsky was in the pay of the Russian State Police as an agent of the Okhrana, but Lenin refused to believe it. In fact, his speeches were often censored by both Lenin and Police Chief Beletsky. Finally, in late 1916, while he was an obscure prisoner-of-war in a German prison camp, Malinovsky's duplicity was exposed, but only after Lenin and his wife had befriended him with packages of food and taken care of his laundry and other personal matters during his imprisonment.

On August 1, 1914 Germany declared war on Russia and five days later Germany's ally, Austria-Hungary, followed with its declaration of war. Lenin who was living in Cracow (a part of Austria) at the time immediately became an enemy alien and was imprisoned as a spy. But ten days later he was released through the efforts of Victor Adler, an outstanding leader of the Austrian Social Democrat Party, who went directly to the Austrian Minister of Interior in Lenin's behalf. Also through Adler's help he was able to obtain a military pass to travel from Cracow to Vienna and thence to Zurich, Switzerland, where he and his wife, together with Zinoviev and his wife, settled. They were to stay there until the fateful day of April 16, 1917 when he arrived in a German armored car at the Finland Station in Petrograd (formerly St. Petersburg) to change the course of history.

But until that time—while he was in Zurich—he was to reach the lowest point of his volatile career. Deserted by his friends and early followers, without even adequate funds for his modest living, many now looked upon him as a crackpot. Viacheslav Menzhinsky, later to become chief of the Soviet secret police, was to write in "Echo", a Paris émigré newspaper, "Lenin has become completely confused—this illegitimate child of Russian absolutism considers himself. . .to be the natural successor to the Russian throne. . .the Leninists are not even a faction. . .(they) hope to drown the voice of the proletariat with their screams. . .and be the drivers of the proletariat." In January 1917, Lenin was hardly known inside Russia except to a few revolutionaries. And to the Socialists of Western Europe he was merely a café conspirator—yet within three months he had installed himself in the palace of the Tsars and was the thundering voice of the greatest revolution since the French revolution of 1789.

"There is no doubt that the fate of every revolution at a certain point is decided by a break in the disposition of the army," Leon Trotsky wrote in "The History of the Russian Revolution". The Tsar appeared to be making every effort to prove Trotsky's thesis a correct one, as he drafted 14 million men into the army and then gave them only 4,100 machine guns to fight with and hardly any light artillery. Staff officers were not only abysmally ignorant of modern military science, they didn't even have the good sense not to send men into battle without any arms whatsoever. The only hope such a man had was if he could get a rifle from a fallen comrade. In fact, there was little cooperation between Generals at the front because they were more interested in their own careers and the petty rivalries involving them than the outcome of a battle. Much of this stemmed from the crushing defeat and demoralization Russia suffered at the hands of the Japanese ten years earlier.

By 1915, 2 million Russian soldiers had been killed or wounded and 1,300,000 had been taken prisoner by the German and Austro-Hungarian forces. In a vain effort to stem the tide, Tsar Nicholas assumed personal command at the front in September 1915, thus giving the drunkard-monk Rasputin unlimited power, through the Empress, to rule Russia. This he did until his assassination in December 1916 at the hands of a group of noblemen who poisoned his food and wine, then riddled his body with bullets and tossed it into the Neva River before his life finally expired. By January 1917, with over 1 million deserters roaming in the rear, the Russian army had all but ceased to exist as a fighting unit.

Meanwhile, the situation at home was deteriorating as fast as the war front. Strikes, bread riots and general chaos reigned. When troops were called on to disperse with bullets an unruly crowd in the capital city of Petrograd, they refused to fire a shot and ended by fraternizing with the demonstrators. It was clearly evident that the 215,000 soldiers stationed in and around the city and 80,000 sailors of the Baltic fleet would no longer support the monarchy. Then Tsar Nicholas removed the last barrier between himself and the revolution when he issued a decree dissolving the Duma on March 11.

But the Duma refused to obey the monarch's orders and appointed a Provisional Government of moderate complexion headed by Prince Georgi E. Lvov as Prime Minister, Paul N. Milyukov as Foreign Minister and Alexander F. Kerensky as Minister of Justice. The real power, however, lay outside the governmental structure and in the hands of a newly created alliance called the Petrograd Soviet of Workers' and Soldiers' Deputies. They controlled all the vital instruments of power—the troops, the communications and transport facilities. On March 15, Tsar Nicholas was forced to resign. At the same time the Petrograd Soviet gave full recognition to the Provisional Government when it promised a program of general amnesty for all political prisoners and exiles; freedom of speech, press, assembly and the right to strike; abolition of all classes and the election of a Constituent Assembly to determine the future form of government and the adoption of a Constitution for Russia. It failed to meet two of the most burning issues, however— the continuation of the war and the redistribution of land. Chkheidze was elected chairman and Kerensky vice-chairman of the Petrograd Soviet of Workers' and Soldiers' Deputies.

No one could have been more surprised by this turn of events and the sudden overthrow of Tsar Nicholas than Lenin and the other political exiles. Soon all roads led to Petrograd—exiles from America, Europe and the vast wastelands of Siberia. And history has no more quixotic and surprising twist than the spectacle of Lenin, a political outcast with few friends or followers, returning to his homeland in the sealed armored car of the enemy (some even thought he was a German agent) in temporary triumph. Soon he was to be disavowed by his fellow Bolsheviks and disowned by all revolutionaries. "Let him live outside the Revolution," Chkheidze

said. Yet within six months this stubborn, political op-
portunist, often accused of being an anarchist, was the
unquestioned leader of the Revolution and dictator of the
proletariat—but only after four more months of furtive
hiding in Petrograd and Finland to avoid arrest by the
Provisional Government.

Soon after the new Provisional Government
gained power, Pravda resumed publication. By early
spring, under the new direction of Stalin, Kamenev and
Muranov, it had assumed a more conciliatory attitude toward the new government. But Lenin and Trotsky continued to attack it vehemently, particularly for its failure
to end the war with Germany. It was on this basis—the
hope that Lenin could aid in a peaceful settlement—that
the Germans, without the concurrence of the Petrograd
Soviet, had granted Lenin the privilege of crossing Germany in a sealed train to the Baltic port of Sassnitz. From
there they took a ferry to Sweden and then the night
train to Stockholm, and then another train for the 600
mile trip to the Swedish-Finnish border, finally arriving
at the Finland Station in Petrograd at 11:10 P.M., April
16, 1917.

Forewarned by notices in Pravda and Bolshevik placards which were carried earlier in the day
throughout the industrial suburbs saying "Lenin arrives
today. Meet him.", Lenin was greeted as a conquering
hero by the thousands awaiting his arrival in the station
courtyard. As he stepped from his coach, the band struck

up the "Marseillaise", not yet knowing the "Internationale", and thundered "such a powerful, stirring and hearty 'hurrah' as I have never heard before in my life," one observer wrote. "Lenin came, or rather ran, into the Tsar's waiting room, wearing a round hat, his face frozen with cold and carrying a magnificent bouquet of flowers." There to officially greet him was the Chairman of the Petrograd Soviet, Chkheidze, a picture of despair (Trotsky said "he was a little afraid of Lenin"). Whether he was afraid of Lenin or not, Chkheidze had every reason to look and act downhearted. He himself had risen from a sickbed that afternoon to bury his son.

Nevertheless, in an impassioned plea for unity, Chkheidze admonished Lenin to take up the "principle task of the revolutionary democracy (which is) to defend our revolution from every kind of attack both from within and without. . .what is needed is not disunity but the closing of the ranks of the entire democracy. . .we hope you will pursue these aims together with us." Any one else might have accepted this welcome with grace and a crowd-pleasing polite reply, waiting for another and better day to propound his political philosophy of extremism. But not Lenin.

All but ignoring Chkheidze and his plea for unity, Lenin looked out beyond the delegates of the executive committee there to welcome him as if to say today's events were of no moment. Then, with piercing eyes and a rasping voice, he shouted the clarion call for a world-wide socialist revolution, of which this was to be just the beginning. Meanwhile the crowd of soldiers and sailors who had been waiting patiently outside could no longer contain themselves. Throwing open the station doors, they broke into the imperial waiting room, grabbed up Lenin and carried him out into the open station square. There, in the glare of searchlights, bands playing, and every one shouting his name, Lenin mounted an armored car. With his head bared and his coat flung open despite the cold, he threw back his head and attacked the war as "shameful imperialist slaughter" fought by "capitalist robbers". Then he sneered at the Soviet Socialists in the nearby waiting room and all others who were cooperating with the provisional government of "capitalist" ministers. "Long live the world-wide socialist revolution," he shouted as the crowd roared its approval. This was the moment of triumph that Lenin had lived his whole life for, but it was to be a fleeting moment. Within a few days he had so antagonized all his Bolshevik friends that when he asked them for their support, not one of them would promise it.

For now, however, he was in complete command of the Party even though he had saved his real scorn for his friends. Later that night about 30 of them had gathered in Bolshevik headquarters midst the crystal chandeliers and frescoed ceilings of Kshesinskaya Palace, the former home of the mistress of a Russian Grand Duke. It was then after 12:30 A.M. There was the inevi-

table tea and welcoming speeches by the top leaders of
the Paty, interrupted by numerous balcony appearances
and short speeches by Lenin to the crowd below.

Once the crowd had dispersed, he gathered his
friends inside and placed them in a half circle in front of
him while he stood against the wall and proceeded to
castigate them for being temporizers. In fact, they were
not much better than traitors to the revolutionary cause,
he said, as he called for the destruction of the Provisional
Government. All power must pass to the Soviets who
should no longer be called Social Democrats but Communists; all the land and the banks should be national-
ized and the land of the aristocrats confiscated. "The
people need peace; the people need bread; the people
need land. . .and they give you war, hunger and no
bread. . .we must fight to the end, until the complete
victory of the proletariat," he told them. "He kept hammering, hammering, hammering and at last he made
them his captives," reported the brilliant journalist Sukhanov. As dawn rose and the meeting broke up, "I felt as
though I had been beaten about the head with flails,"
Sukhanov said.

Lenin, for the time being at least, had complete
mastery over the Party. At the same time the Provisional
Government was lulled into a false sense of security
thinking that the assistance he had received from the
Germans together with his advocacy of peace would destroy him. The next morning at a general conference of
Social Democrat leaders in the Tauride Palace, Lenin

reiterated the hard line he had laid down the night before
to the Bolsheviks, thus forever destroying any hopes for
party unity. During the meeting Lenin was attacked as
an anarchist by the Mensheviks, comparing him to the
renowned anarchist, Bakunin. This so angered the Bolsheviks that they bolted the meeting and Lenin, who
could never accept the criticism he gave others, left with
them.

Krupskaya was in tears—only the night before
he had been hailed as a hero; now he was an outcast. "Let
him live outside the revolution, while we—the rest of
us—continue along the revolutionary road," Chkheidze,
who was presiding, remarked as Lenin left the room.
What had so angered the general conference was Lenin's
enunciation of the now famous "April Theses" which he
had composed in note form after awaking at 10:00 A.M.
the morning after his arrival in Petrograd and after only a
few hours sleep. The "Theses" called for nothing less
than civil war and the destruction of the Russian state as
it then existed: abolition of parliament, the bureaucracy
and the police; confiscation of all landed estates; abolition
of all banks except one to be under the control of the
Soviet Workers' Deputies; seizure of all means of production; and the transfer of all power to the proletariat. In
short, what he proposed was a dictatorship of the proletariat, but he concealed his purpose from the masses and
even his own general staff by the use of the general
phrase "All power to the Soviets".

Two days later the "April Theses" were published in full in Pravda and at the same time were denounced by its editor, Kamenev. No Bolshevik organization thereafter would identify itself with them and even Lenin's closest comrades refused their support when Lenin asked them for it. Yet within one month, when the all-Russian Bolshevik Party conference was held from May 7 to May 12, 1917, Lenin was again in complete control and the "April Theses" were accepted as the foundation work for their principal resolutions. Sukhanov wrote, "It never occurred to us that Lenin would not depart by an inch from these abstractions. Still less did it occur to us that he would be able to conquer not only the revolution, not only all its active participants, not only the entire Soviet, but even his own Bolsheviks."

What Lenin sensed, and the others didn't, was that after 300 years of Romanov rule the discontent of the soldiers, sailors and the peasant masses was so overwhelming that the revolution had not spent itself, nor the desire for violence. Yet the Provisional government under Prince Lvov as Prime Minister and Kerensky as Minister of War continued to hold its meetings in the Prince's unguarded apartment despite the raging violence. And it continued to issue vapid pleas for some kind of a nebulous democratic faith to a populace that knew nothing of democracy but seethed with resentment against the whole bourgeois world whatever its ruling caste. In reality anarchy had overtaken Russia as it became beset with arbitrary arrests, lootings, workingmen on strike, soldiers deserting, mobs burning down manor houses or looking for any trouble or mischief they could find. The government reigned but did not rule. Long before, Kerensky, with great prescience, had said to Lenin "When you, in alliance with reaction, shall destroy our power, then you will have a real dictator."

Lenin's followers throughout that turbulent summer numbered only a fractional part of the 15,000 known Bolsheviks in the city of Petrograd with a population of 2 million. His enemies were numerous and had organized a brilliant smear campaign against him, especially among the soldiers who marched through the streets demanding his arrest as a traitor and his expulsion to Germany. Still he and his small band of agitators persisted in hammering away at the simple thesis of: all power to the Soviets, land to the peasants, worker control of the factories and an end to the capitalist war and capitalist rule. Gradually their propaganda won over most of the working classes, even to the point where in July Lenin lost control over the left-wing extremists in the party who engineered a two-day abortive revolt. Whereupon on July 19 the Provisional Government ordered the arrest of Lenin and other Bolshevik leaders. Nothing came of it, however, because both sides were afraid of antagonizing other non-Bolshevik Socialists and all effective police action had been destroyed by the March Revolution anyway.

On July 21 Prince Lvov resigned as Prime Minister and Kerensky succeeded him. Lenin fled to Finland and Kerensky appointed General Kornilov commander-

in-chief of the army. On September 7 Kornilov tried to
seize the reins of government but failed and was dis-
missed by Kerensky. Thereafter Kerensky, having no
military or police power, was completely dependent on
the Petrograd Soviet for his power base. All Bolshevik
leaders who had been arrested were now released. Lenin
returned to the city on October 23 and immediately persuaded the leadership of the Bolshevik Party to seek an
armed insurrection against the Kerensky government.
One of the disruptive effects of Kornilov's failure to overcome the Kerensky government showed itself in the discipline of the army. The ordinary soldier now knew that
he no longer had to obey the commands of his superiors.
It was but a short step from this for Trotsky and Lenin,
who had organized a Military Revolutionary Committee
to carry out the coup d'état, to appoint a Bolshevik commissar to every army unit in Petrograd. Their orders
were to see that only the commands of the Committee
were carried out.

On the day before the Bolshevik uprising Lenin
was in hiding in the apartment of one Margarita Fofanova when he wrote the Central Committee of the party,
"any delay in the insurrection is like unto death. . . . It is
necessary at all costs, this evening, tonight to arrest the
members of the government, to disarm (vanquish, if they
resist) the officer cadets and others." Then, sensing the
urgency of this historical moment, he said "We must not
wait. We may lose everything."

That same day (November 5—new style) Kerensky unwittingly decided to cooperate with the revolution by ordering a battalion of shock troops to proceed on the capital. Their orders were to cut all telephone lines to Bolshevik headquarters, the Smolny, a three-story building formerly used as a school for the daughters of the nobility, and to demolish the presses of Bolshevik newspaper, Rabuchy Put. Word of these plans reached Trotsky, who had assumed command of the Revolutionary Military Committee, the next morning. Immediately he ordered a company of the Lithuanian regiment to surround the newspaper to insure its publication and guards to be placed around the Smolny.

The revolution had started, but Lenin neither knew it nor was he privy to any of its planning. Yet that same morning (November 6) he wrote the last of his many letters to the Military Revolutionary Committee frantically urging an immediate start to the revolution. "We must not wait! We may lose everything!" he wrote. "Who should take power? This is not important at the moment. Let the Military Committee take it . . . the matter must definitely be decided this evening or tonight . . . revolutionaries would be committing an immeasurable crime if they let this moment pass . . . the government is tottering. It must be given the final push at all costs. Delay in starting is death."

It was obvious that Lenin was acutely aware that the historical moment was at hand. It was not only the time of the greatest vulnerability of the Provisional government, but there were rumors that at any time

France and Britain would make a separate peace with Germany and turn their forces against the revolutionaries. He was also concerned that the all-Russian Congress (of Soviets), which was to meet any day now, would be too unwieldy an organization to take any swift and decisive action. And then there were other top-ranking Bolsheviks, including Kamanev and Zinoviev, who were either opposed to the revolution or thought its timing premature. Only Trotsky agreed with Lenin and said later "If we had not seized power (then), we would not have seized it at all." Even Lenin's personal life might not have been the same—and he might never had assumed the unquestioned personal command of the revolution— if he had not taken that long walk from his hideaway in the Vyborg district to the Smolny that night at considerable risk to his life, as he did.

　　　Fofanova returned from her job at the publisher's office late in the afternoon and told Lenin that most of the bridges to the inner city had been raised. To Lenin this posed a critical situation; if Kerensky could raise all the bridges to the inner city of Petrograd, the revolution would fail because everything depended on capturing the inner city. He would not know until late that evening that all ten bridges leading from the working class headquarters to Petrograd had been quietly captured. At 9:00 P.M. Fofanova returned with the news that now all the bridges were in the hands of the revolutionaries. Still he had had no word from the Military Revolutionary Committee as to what was happening or even what their plans

were. He did not know they had already decided to
strike at 2:00 A.M. He was merely told the time was not
ripe for him to leave his hiding place.

At 9:30 P.M. he dispatched Fofanova to the
Smolny with an urgent request for details of their plans
for the uprising. He said he would wait until 11:00 P.M.
for her to return and if she didn't come by then, he
would do as he pleased. Pacing the floor over and over
again, he weighed the risks of making the trip to the
Smolny. He would have to walk because the street cars
had stopped running, and there was every chance he
would be shot upon recognition. If the bridges were up,
he would have to hire a boat to cross the river Neva, and
then the cadets would discover him with their searchlights playing on the river.

At the same time he could not understand why
the revolt had been started without him or at least why
there had not been some effort to contact him. He was
tormented by the idea that important information had
been withheld from him. After all, it would have been
easy enough for them to have sent an armored car for him
or a guard of Red escorts—but nothing had been done at
all. Hurt, dejected but mad he decided nothing would be
gained by staying where he was, outside the mainstream
of events, with others assuming the mantle of leadership
in a revolution which he considered his brainchild. So
putting a wig on his head and tying a large handkerchief
around his face, he instructed his Finnish companion,
Eino Rahja, to tell anyone who stopped them that he

could not talk because he had a toothache. Then he scribbled a note to Fofanova saying, "I have gone where you did not want me to go. Au revoir, Ilyich."

It was a cold, windy night as Lenin put on his galoshes thinking it might rain. Fortunately there was no snow. Slowly and in silence they made their way through the Vyborg district without incident. And with great luck they were able to catch the last streetcar on its way to the depot. Taking it as far as they could, they left it and walked the rest of the way until they reached the Vyborg bridge, which, to their surprise, was open to traffic. It was their first anxious moment, but the Red Guards at the bridge suspected nothing as they eyed these two typical proletarians dressed in workmen's clothes, and let them pass without questioning. However, as they approached the other side of the bridge a solitary cadet moved toward them and might have detained them had not some Red Guards come along at the same time to engage him in conversation, letting Lenin and Rahja slip by in safety. Thus more than half the journey had been accomplished without trouble, but the most difficult part was to come.

As they were making their way down the Shpalernaya, out of nowhere appeared two mounted cadets who demanded to see their passes. "Go ahead, I'll deal with them," Rahja whispered to Lenin. Then, as Lenin proceeded ahead, Rahja acted the part of a drunken rowdy. To all questions about a pass, he replied that he did not know what they were talking about, even after one of the cadets flailed him across the head with a nagaika. At first they thought of arresting him but finally decided there was no point in arresting a common drunk when there was so much else to do, and let him go.

The rest of the trip to the Smolny was accomplished without incident except for one final indignity to the future leader of the Russian state. Because their passes were white and new passes had been issued in red, they were refused admission. For ten minutes they argued heatedly with the guards, but to no avail as the pushing, shouting crowd behind them grew more and more restive. Finally, unable to be contained any longer, the crowd surged forward carrying Lenin and Rahja past the guards who stood helpless before the onrushing humanity. "You see, our side always wins," Lenin said with a satisfied smile to Rahja.

Unrecognized by anyone in the milling throngs in the Smolny and being unfamiliar with the building, Lenin found his way upstairs and sat down by a window while Rahja went in search of Trotsky. Soon Trotsky sent word to Lenin that he and the Military Revolutionary Committee would see him in room 100. There Trotsky explained that the military operations were already under way and that by morning all the strong points in the city would be in their hands without firing a shot. At 1:00 A.M. the first Red Guards started their operation and by morning the Bolsheviks had captured the post office, telephone exchange, telegraph agency, all power stations, the national bank and the last of the bridges remaining in enemy hands. All the railroad stations except the Finland Station had been seized. By daybreak even the streetcars were running again and all bridges were open to traffic. "Everything happened with fabulous ease," Sukhanov, the journalist, wrote. It was as if nothing had had happened at all; everything was so normal and quiet.

That afternoon Trotsky stepped before a meeting of the Petrograd Soviet and declared the Provisional Government had been overthrown without "a single casualty" (this was not entirely correct). He was greeted with wild applause. Lenin, Zinoviev and Lunacharsk were also introduced and made short speeches which were received with polite, perfunctory applause. Obviously, Trotsky was the hero of the hour. Later that night the new government was constituted and authorized to rule until the convocation of the Constituent Assembly. Again Lenin, with his steel will and rapier-like mind, was able to "conquer not only the revolution (but) all its active participants" and get himself appointed President of the Soviet of People's Commissars, with L. D. Bronstein (Trotsky) as Commissar for Foreign Affairs and I. V. Dzhugashvili (Stalin) as Commissar for Nationalities.

Everyone knew that the real power lay in the hands of Lenin and Trotsky, not Stalin, and if Lenin had not taken that lonely, dangerous, fateful walk in a revolution-racked city the night of November 6, the power might have been Trotsky's alone.

EPILOGUE

On November 25, the elections to the Constituent Assembly were held with the following results: out of 707 deputies elected, the Social Revolutionaries won 370 seats (a majority), the Bolsheviks 175, the pro-Lenin left Socialist Revolutionaries 40, the Mensheviks 16, the Popular-Socialists 2, the Cadets 17. There were 86 elected from various minority groups and 11 without any party affiliation. The vote was clearly for moderate Socialism and against Lenin. So the day after the Assembly convened, January 18, 1918, Lenin had it abolished and at the same time the Electoral Commission placed under arrest. Lenin had favored it as long as it could be used against Kerensky, but when it couldn't be simply had it abolished. He was consistent in only one thing—in being a professional revolutionist and in devoting his entire life to the proletarian revolution. To him mercy was a useless, bourgeois virtue. "There are no morals in politics; there is only expediency," he said.

Toward the end of 1921, Lenin began complaining of increasing insomnia and general tiredness and more frequent headaches. A few months later he suffered an attack of vertigo. In the early part of May 1922 he had his first stroke which resulted in a temporary loss of speech and the use of his right arm and leg. By July, however, he was on his feet again occupying the seat of

power in Moscow, the new capital. He even appeared
before the fourth Congress of the Comintern but broke
down during a speech before it.

On November 25, 1922 he was forced to stop
all work and in December he suffered his second stroke.
By then he had relinquished all political power to a triumvirate of Zinoviev, Kamenev and Stalin, all of whom
opposed Trotsky. Years later, in the famous purge trials
during the 1930's, Stalin was to have Zinoviev and
Kamenev executed for treason. Of Stalin, Lenin would
write in January 3, 1923: "He is too rude . . . to be General Secretary of the Party" and should be removed. In
March he was struck by his third stroke and was taken to
his country home in Gorki, a suburb of Moscow. There
on January 21, 1924, he had his fourth and final stroke.
In April he would have been 54 years of age. The autop-
sy was performed by Professor Rozanov who said "we
found a massive sclerosis of the cerebral vessels—the
amazing thing was not that the thinking power remained
intact in such a sclerotic brain, but that he could live so
long with such a brain."

He had served as head of state for only five
years, but he had been a revolutionist, in exile mostly,
for a quarter of a century, always "hammering, hammering, hammering" with a determination that brooked
no opposition. Yet there were probably only two "moments" in his turbulent life that stand out. One was
when he arrived at the Finland Station in Petrograd,

April 16, 1917, and castigated his fellow Soviets for cooperating with the Socialists in the Provisional Government. Thus he appealed to the hunger of the crowds for
food and peace (and violence) and placed himself in the
forefront of the revolutionaries seeking the total capitulation of the government. The other was the night of November 6 when he was all but excluded from the planning and execution of the revolution itself, the night he
took that long and dangerous walk from his hiding place
to the Smolny, headquarters of the revolution, to assume
control of the Bolshevik Party and the Russian State. It
is quite possible had he not taken that fateful walk,
Trotsky, who was in control, would have become the
dominant figure in the revolution and its history, not
Lenin.

VI
THE MOMENT-
CHANCE OR
DESTINY?

The Moment—Chance or Destiny?

IT IS NOT always the most prominent person nor the most dramatic moment which is involved.

In December 1974, Bart Starr, who in the late 60's had quarterbacked two Super Bowl championship Green Bay Packer football teams under the great Vince Lombardi, was chosen the new coach of the Packers. Now a successful businessman content with life as it was, he was asked to take the position when the fortunes of the Packers were at their lowest ebb. When he was asked by the press why he was doing it, he quoted Winston Churchill: "To every man comes in his lifetime that special moment when he is figuratively tapped on the shoulder and offered that chance to do a very special thing unique to him and fitted to his talents. What a tragedy if that moment finds him unprepared or unqualified for that work."

"I firmly believe that," Starr said. "I'm not as qualified as I'd like to be, but I'm willing." He was 41. He didn't say that Churchill was 66 when he was "figuratively tapped on the shoulder" to become Prime Minister of Great Britain in the time of her greatest need and during her "finest hour."

As we look back over our examples and reflect on this age factor, we are struck by the fact that in practically every case "the moment" came to the individual by middle age or at least when he or she was in his forties or less—and some in their childhood. And sometimes the "moment" came and went unnoticed because it did not lead to immediate success. This may lead the reader to doubt our premise that there is a precise "moment" in most of our lives from which all else in our life flows. But to us it means simply that there is no scientific guide to lead us to that moment. Chance, or call it destiny, may play the most significant part, with one very important qualification, the will of the person involved. Underlying the chance or destiny factor is the intuition, sometimes the dedication and, above all else, one's will which, in fact, may itself bring the chance or destiny factor into play. How else can one explain the actions of a five-year old Sarah Bernhardt throwing herself out of a window to free herself from the slums of Paris to gain an education? Or of Anne Sullivan at 14 pleading for her freedom from being institutionalized for life and gaining it? Or of a Booker T. Washington who at 16 scrubbed a recreation room floor so well he was admitted to college.

Perhaps they didn't know exactly where their actions would lead—any more than Alfred I. du Pont did as he stood astride the boardroom door, or Jones when he

decided on that iron shot at Inwood, or Cronin when he
recovered his manuscript from the ash heap, or Lenin as
he hammered desperately and obsessively away at Revolution. But as adults, their will and dedication knew no
bounds. They must have felt that somehow chance or
destiny would favor them if they only persisted. Only
Wilson faced his greatest moment with serenity as he let
his fate be played out in the hands of his convention managers. Even after his devastating stroke in October 1919,
Wilson "preserved a remarkable serenity and detachment
because of his confidence in Providence and the goodness
and wisdom of God," his biographer, Arthur Stanley
Link of Princeton University, would write. One has the
feeling that only Caesar truly chartered his course and
knew where it would take him—until he reached the
Rubicon and destiny took over.

    One wonders if it is not good hindsight that
tells the principal (and the author) when the moment oc-
curs. Nine years ago young six year old Matt Winkler of
Columbus, Ohio, was bitten by a rabid bat in his home.
Two thousand years of medical history said he would
die, and die a horrible death with convulsions and chok-
ing. It was October 10, 1970 when it happened. Four
days later the public health authorities reported the bat
was rabid. Immediately a series of 14 daily painful injec-
tions of rabies vaccine began. By November 1, there
were still no dangerous signs although Matt's mother said
the boy was beginning to "drift off" before his bedtime.
November 14 his condition became quite serious when

his speech became garbled and his left side stiffened as he lost all sense of coordination. Then he fell into a partial coma.

Dr. Michael Hattwick had arrived from the Rabies Center of the Atlanta Center for Communicable Disease Control. He was convinced Matt didn't have to die. He said people so afflicted had died in the past because they "gave up." The doctors said they would die; so they did. His theory was that it was not the disease which killed them; it was the symptoms—symptoms which occurred in other diseases too. His plan was to treat every symptom as it appeared. The crisis came when Matt's heartbeat and breathing raced out of control. The doctor did a tracheotomy to ease his breathing. Then his left hand started to open and close convulsively and they gave him anti-convulsants. The pediatrician on the case, Dr. Thomas T. Weis, said when the breathing difficulty arose "we were expecting something worse. Instead the boy began to improve. We didn't recognize the turning point *until after we passed it*." On January 27, 1971, three months after his ordeal began, Matt was released by his doctors. He thus became the first person on record to survive the horrors of rabies. Because of him and because one doctor refused to accept death as the answer, countless other victims now have a chance at life.

But it is not always hindsight. Sometimes it is "lateral thinking", as the philosophers call it, a process whereby the mind scans seemingly unrelated events and facts and finds new meaning where none seemed to exist before. Sir Alexander Fleming, an English bacteriologist, noticed that bacterial colonies on old discarded agar plates were disintegrating next to an old mold which often developed on these plates. This had happened thousands of times before and thousands of bacteriologists and technicians had seen it happen without giving it any further thought, but it was the prepared mind and genius of the moment of Dr. Fleming which recognized the relationship and theorized, correctly, that it was the mold that inhibited the bacterial growth, and thus penicillin was discovered.

Or it could be the element of surprise which pervades human life and its history—the "fecundity of the unexpected," as Proudhon termed it. Historians are "hunters of causes", the noted British historian J.H. Plumb has said—when often there are no causes to be found. Why, he asks, was there a worldwide feeling of revulsion against slavery in the mid-nineteenth century which led to its abolition in Europe, the West Indies and America when the institution of slavery had been accepted unreservedly since Neolithic times (10,000 B.C.)? And who could have predicted the world-wide acceptance and success of Christianity and Islam. There was no greater surprise than Jesus Christ himself who in his teachings, especially the Sermon on the Mount, contradicted a whole world of customs and values. Indeed, Plumb states, one of the greatest surprises of our time may be a very sharp decline (already started) in the world's population growth over the next century. Then he recalls another period of history and asks, "Why did Elizabethan Englishmen want babies and Stuart Englishmen not?"

A key element in any "surprise" is the inspiration which accompanies it. It is the intuitive insight or inspiration which, according to the eminent historian, Barbara W. Tuchman, leads one to the "moment of synthesis". It was such a moment with the famous naval historian, Admiral Alfred T. Mahan, when he realized that it was "Hannibal's failure to control the sea communications with Carthage (that) the idea flashed on him of the influence of sea power on history." From that time on he would know that sea power was a major factor in international politics and not just a series of naval campaigns and technical studies. "The integrating idea or insight evolves from the internal logic of the material in the course of putting it together," Mrs. Tuchman concluded.

Arnold Toynbee said the "right moment" was even related to his work of writing: "In work of every kind, including intellectual work, there comes the right moment for taking action. There is no instrument that will tell one when that moment has arrived; one has to sense it by intuition and the right timing will be different in every case. But to hit upon it is indispensible for success; and to delay too long can be just as fatal as to act precipitately can be. The effect of wrong timing, either way, will be to aggravate the imperfection that is inherent in any human activity."

But if "the moment" so often has to be sensed by intuition, isn't it possible that mere chance or destiny plays a part in it, both for the individual and perhaps for nations? Was it chance or destiny that gave us a man crippled by polio who knew no fear and told us we had "nothing to fear but fear itself" in the depths of the Great Depression, Franklin D. Roosevelt; or a sad Mr. Lincoln who faced political extinction as a Congressman when he voted against our war with Mexico but as President fought a war which saved the Union; or a Washington who saved a nation with his courage at Valley Forge and his luck at Yorktown—a sudden storm which prevented the escape of Cornwallis, which in turn led to the final surrender of the British.

"There is a turning point in every nation, a critical moment when it has the power to turn back a force from without or a corrosion from within," The Most Reverend Fulton J. Sheen noted recently. "It has been called 'a time of visitation' when power is given to vanquish, but if not seized, turns the nation into a kind of cadaver on which the scavengers feed." In early 1781 the American military fortunes under George Washington were at their lowest ebb. Not only was the Continental Treasury empty and its currency worthless, but as enlistments expired, the hungry, unpaid men drifted back to their farms. It could be said that there was no American army at all. Only two pockets of strength were left—one a French force of 5,000 men at Newport, R.I. under General de Rochambeau and the other Washington's own army of 3,000 stationed near West Point, N.Y.

Washington was sick of being on the defensive and yearned for just one victory. At first he thought of combining forces with the French for an attack on Sir Henry Clinton's well-equipped army of 14,500 holding New York City, but quickly gave this up when his advance detachments were attacked by British foraging parties. Next he turned his attention to the 5,000 man army of Cornwallis at Yorktown, Virginia. Encouraged by word that the French fleet under Comte de Grasse with 30 vessels and 3,000 men stationed in the West Indies was prepared to aid in an assault on Yorktown, he decided to combine forces with Rochambeau and make an all-out attack on Yorktown. They were to steal secretly across eastern Pennsylvania and New Jersey while a small fleet under Admiral Barras brought the artillery down from Newport. All were to join together with De Grasse in the Chesapeake in September for the final assault.

Their efforts were graced by two strokes of good fortune. First, Clinton in New York failed to notice their departure and second, Admiral Rodney, commander of the British Atlantic fleet, tired and in poor health, did not choose to spend another winter in the cold north Atlantic—even though he had been warned that De

Grasse was moving his fleet northward. Thus, he relinquished all control of the sea lanes to the French. By early September De Grasse was safely lodged within the capes of the Chesapeake awaiting the arrival of Barras' ships with the artillery from New York and by the end of the month the armies of Washington and Rochambeau had been ferried from Baltimore and Annapolis to establish the siege of Yorktown.

Now Cornwallis was surrounded on three sides by superior forces. Still he refused to ask for help from Clinton. His fourth side was the south bank of the York River from which he hoped to make his escape. His only hope was that the besiegers would be too busy digging their ramparts to take notice of the small boats he would use to cross the river. If he made the crossing safely, he would then march northward, unencumbered by heavy artillery and baggage, to join forces with Clinton in New York.

Under cover of darkness on the night of October 16, Cornwallis began his movement of troops across the York River. By midnight a sizeable number had accomplished the task, and everything seemed to be going according to plan. Then, without warning, destiny played its fickle hand, and there arose from nowhere a furious storm which overturned the boats, drove others helplessly down the river and prevented those who had reached the opposite shore from returning. The next day, realizing that all hope for escape was now gone,

Cornwallis offered his surrender. The war was not over, but it was the beginning of the end. King George III now knew that a large area of the continent was forever freed of British control and that any further loss would drive the Americans and French into closer alliance, all to the increasing detriment of the larger interests of the British Empire. Soon he was to summon back into power those ministers who had been most friendly to the American cause—Rockingham, Shelburne and Fox. Within six months the man most responsible for the revolution, Prime Minister Lord North, had resigned. And within a year a provisional treaty of peace was signed in Paris. After eight years of war, and untold hardships, when the future was darkest, luck, destiny, chance—the fury of a storm—had turned the tide of war in favor of the young American colonies—at a cost of only fifty-two killed and one hundred and thirty-four wounded, mostly Frenchmen.

Was it the alchemy of the fates or the stubborn refusal to accept defeat that prompted Columbus to drive his mutinous crew into the unknown vastness of the Atlantic and the discovery of a new world? It was October 10, 1492, thirty days and 3,000 miles westward from the Canary Islands, when the restive crew realized they had long passed the position where Columbus had predicted land would be found in his search for a new route to the riches of the Orient. It had been a quiet voyage with fair winds and calm seas. Only Columbus, one of the best navigators of his time, knew that they not only had passed that position but had already doubled any previous record for ocean navigation. And it was all done by dead reckoning with only the aid of a compass, a feat which would surpass the ability of many modern-day sailing vessels of equal size with the most sophisticated instrumentation. Columbus himself was bewildered because he fully expected Japan to lie only 2,500 miles to the west of the Canaries. But he would reveal none of this to his mutinous crew who now demanded that he turn back. Just two more days, he would plead with them, and then if land wasn't sighted, he would turn back. Anyway, there was no use in thinking about it now since unfavorable trade winds and a rising sea had set in. Sullen but pacified, they sailed on.

History will always wonder whether it was the stubborn, even unthinking, determination of the man or the demand of the circumstances which prompted Columbus' great discovery. Or luck—within hours the first favorable sign appeared when birds were sighted overhead, indicating that land might not be far off. And now there was a full moon in a cloudless sky which meant that if their landfall came at night they would not miss it. Two days later at 2 a.m. on October 12, 1492 under a brisk trade wind and the heaviest following sea of the entire voyage, Rudrigo de Triana, lookout on the Pinta's forecastle, saw something like a white sand cliff gleaming in the moonlight. "Tierra, Tierra," he shouted, and what is now known as San Salvador in the Bahamas became the first land ever sighted in the Western Hemisphere by a European since the days of the northmen.

Columbus was not the only man in his time who thought that lands existed across the unchartered oceans to the west of Europe, but it was his daring, persistence, dedication and expert seamanship—and luck— that proved it to be so. At 41, this was the high watermark of his career. The rest of his life was spent in failure and frustration. For the next fourteen years and three more voyages he only proved his ineptitude as a colonial administrator for the Spanish Royal Court. Finally the monarchs lost all faith in his ability to find either gold or a new passage to Japan and the Orient, and they cast him out. He died in neglect and all but forgotten. His moment had been October 10, 1492, when he decided not to turn back.

> *"It could very well be that the life of every person is not so much decided by the routine events of everyday, but rather during two or three great moments of decision which happen in every life."*
> *The Most Reverend Fulton J. Sheen*

The moment may be so mundane as to be hidden in the college we decide to attend or the person we marry or even the day we decide to be honest or dishonest. And it can lead to success or failure or something in between. For the ambitious Mary Todd Lincoln it was what she saw, and others didn't, in the tall, ungainly, homely young lawyer from Springfield, Ill. which led her to the White House. And it was the tragedy of witnessing the assassination of her husband and the death of three of her four sons which led to her trial for insanity, at the instigation of her only remaining son, Robert, and institutionalization for one year.

For Florence Nightingal it was the decision *not* to marry. The brilliant and pretty Miss Nightingal, daughter of a wealthy British family, was educated in higher mathematics, music, art, science, literature, Italian, French, German, all of which she spoke fluently—all in all, "a capital young lady," Sir Henry de la Beche would say. But it was not enough. She was bored by the after-dinner snoring of Lord Melborne in the royal presence and the applauding of Prince Albert for his imaginary skills at billiards.

"Father, Mother, I am going to be a nurse," she announced one day when she was thirty years old. "Why, you're insane," they said, as they reminded her that nursing (in the mid-nineteenth century) was regarded as among the lowest of professions; in fact, so low that when prostitutes were brought into court, they were given the choice of either going to prison or taking on hospital work. "I am at the age when Christ began his mission," she would confide to her diary . . . (there shall be) "no more childish things, no more vain things, no more love, no more marriage." And there weren't. Florence Nightingal became the mother of modern nursing.

Jane Addams was also the daughter of a wealthy man, a miller from Cedarville, Ill. and she wanted to be a doctor. It was while studying at the Women's Medical College of Philadelphia in 1881 that a congenital problem of curvature of the spine laid her so low her doctor prescribed extended rest and a trip to Europe. Along towards midnight one night while she was sightseeing on a bus in the East End of London, the vehicle stopped beside a traveling grocery truck. The truck was surrounded by men and women who could only be described as human derelicts, their tattered clothes barely covering their emaciated bodies, as they shouted their bids of "tupences" for the decayed food being offered at auction from the day's leftovers. She watched unbelievingly as one man bid and received a cabbage that was worm-eaten and rotten, thoroughly unfit for human or animal consumption. Yet he greedily grabbed his "prize" and ran off to a corner by himself where he proceeded to devour all of it in its raw and unwholesome state. For the rest of her London stay Jane Addams would avoid the back streets and alleys of London. She would never return to medical school again.

However, it was not until April of 1888, seven years and several European trips later, that it happened. During the day she had witnessed several bullfights in which five bulls and many horses had been killed. That night she returned to her hotel room "stern and pale with disapproval." "I felt myself tired and condemned, not only by this disgusting experience but by the entire moral situation which it revealed." Suddenly she realized that all her travels and study in Europe were a "defense for continued idleness." "I had fallen into the meanest type of self-deception in making myself believe that all this was in preparation for great things to come . . . nothing less than the moral reaction following the experience of a bullfight had been able to reveal to me . . . that I had been tied to the tail of the veriest oxcart of self-seeking . . . I had made up my mind the next day, whatever happened, I would carry out the plan (eventually the Hull House settlement)."

In January 1889 she returned to Chicago and started looking for a location for the new settlement house. ". . . the period of mere passive receptivity had come to an end, and I had at last finished with the everlasting 'preparation for life', however ill-prepared I might be." Located in the heart of Chicago's foreign-born population, Hull House became a refuge for the sick and hungry among the Poles, Germans, Italians, Jews, Negroes, Russians, Englishmen, Irishmen, Frenchmen, Scandinavians, Bohemians and Swiss and a model for other settlement houses which soon sprang up around the country.

David W. Mitchell wanted to be a veterinarian but the school was located in northern California and his sweetheart lived in southern California. So David Mitchell went to work at age 19 as a mail clerk for Avon Products, Inc. in Pasadena, Calif. which was in the south. Now, thirty-two years later in his early 50's, he is chairman and chief executive officer of the world's largest manufacturer of cosmetics and toiletries (over two billion in sales). But the fact that he even stayed with the company that long was "one of those turns of fate that determine the direction our lives take," he would say. "I had been with the company about six years and a job opened in sales. I applied and was turned down, so I resigned." However, the general manager asked him to stay on so that he would attend a conference while he was working out his notice. Then he "talked me into withdrawing my resignation. I've always been thankful for his interest." Mitchell got his sales job three months later and in 1960 he was named branch manager for the sales office at Morton Grove, Ill. From there he was transferred to the home office in New York City where he gradually rose through several vice-presidencies to president in 1972, chief executive officer in 1976 and chairman in 1977.

James A Gloin majored in English at Butler University in Indianapolis, Ind., but he had a knack for figures. In 1925, when he was 24, he got a job in the research department of L.S. Ayres and Co. in Indianapolis. Many people haven't heard of L.S. Ayres and Co. (now a subsidary of Associated Dry Goods Corp.), but it was then a family-owned department store with the highest of reputations nationally. In fact, it was right at the top of the second tier of department stores in the

United States, just below such familiar names as Macy's of New York, Hudson's of Detroit and Marshall Field's of Chicago. Within four years, by late 1929, Gloin had risen to the position of assistant to the company's comptroller. He was then 28 years of age and had been with the company throughout its greatest period of expansion in the booming 1920's. One day L. Roy Austin, the comptroller, turned to Gloin and said "would you mind going over next year's budget figures with Mr. Ayres for me? It will only take a half hour or an hour and I am really too busy at this time to do it." Gloin nervously agreed. Every one loved Mr. Frederick M. Ayres, the president and son of the founder, who was a kindly but shrewd businessman. But this was an awesome task for a young man even if it did only take "a half hour or an hour."

The day for the budget review arrived and Gloin had hardly settled in a chair in Mr. Ayres' office when the president blurted out, "I suppose you know, young man, things are out of hand here. Now let's go to work and get them together." Gloin was to spend not one hour but two to three every day for the next six weeks carefully and laboriously going over each item in the budget with Mr. Ayres. Within eighteen months he was to become the comptroller, then assistant general manager and treasurer and finally executive vice-president in 1949. In 1962 he became president in which capacity he served until his retirement in February 1966.

But the moment doesn't always have such a

happy ending. For Malcolm Braly, age 14, an orphan, abandoned by his father and mother, it meant a life in and out of prison for eighteen years—all because he stole a boy's overcoat from a laundry. Braly didn't need the coat; it just happened to be the kind his friends were wearing in high school and he didn't have the money to keep up with them the way he wanted. Later one of his classmates recognized the coat Braly was wearing as his own, and reported him. Thus began a life of petty crime and thievery which lasted almost two decades for Malcolm Braly until he found himself and became a successful author.

For Yuri, a moment of weakness became a disaster from which he never recovered. Yuri was a loyal Russian officer with a fine war record who was captured by the Germans in World War II. He spent the first two years of his captivity in a concentration camp near Vilnius. Although he had a superb command of conversational German, he refused to use it for fear he would be made a translator and be forced to betray his fellow prisoners. Instead he posed as an artist and painted acceptable pictures for the commandant's staff. For this he received food which was denied his fellow prisoners, Russian officers who were nothing more than animals "who gnawed the bones of dead horses, baked patties from potatoe rinds and smoked manure," while lice swarmed over their bodies.

"In every life there is one particular event that is decisive for the entire person—for his fate, his con-

victions, his passions," Aleksandr I. Solzhenitsyn said in
relating this story in "Gulag Archipelago." For Yuri it
came in 1943 when, already softened by the relative ease
of his lot as a prisoner, he succumbed further to the demands of the flesh and accepted a commission as a lieu-
tenant in the German Army on the basis of his knowledge of the German language. Now, as an intelligence
officer, he was free to travel throughout Germany out-
fitted in a German uniform. But much of his time was
spent in Berlin visiting with Russian émigrés and drinking more and more vodka.

Occasionally Yuri's fellow prisoners were sent
behind the Russian lines as spies. But once across the line
they would throw away their TNT and radio apparatus
rather than betray their compatriots. And rarely did they
return to the Germans. One day, as the war approached
its end in 1945, one of them did return. The event was
considered so unusual that the Germans assumed that he
had been sent back by Russian counterintelligence and
therefore, should be shot. But Yuri befriended him and
begged the authorities to spare his life, which they did as
an example to encourage others to return. To show his
thanks, the returned "spy" invited Yuri to share a bottle
of vodka with him. As they celebrated and grew warm
with the liquor, his new friend leaned across the table
and said "Yuri Nikolayevich! The Soviet Command
promises you forgiveness if you will come over to us immediately."

Thoughts of returning to his homeland and re-
union with his family were overwhelming, but Yuri said
nothing. For two weeks he wrestled with himself unable
to come to a decision. Then, one day as the Russian of-
fensive penetrated beyond the Vistula river, Yuri led his
small band of spies out of the line of fire and into the
quiet of a Polish farm. There he stopped and ordered
them to gather around him, saying "I am going over to
the Soviet side! There is a free choice for every one!"

The entire "school" hid themselves away on the
farm and waited for the Russian tanks and field forces to
come. When they did, they were followed almost immediately by the Russian counterintelligence group called
SMERSH who seized Yuri and took him off by himself.
For ten days he was interrogated about his experiences in
the German school, its work and sabotage assignments.
When the last bit of useful information had been extract-
ed from Yuri, he was shunted off to a prison camp.
There he was to remain—telling and retelling this story
to his fellow prisoners—until one day, without warning,
he was removed from his cell, never to be heard from
again. For Yuri it was not his gullibility in believing the
Russians would accept him back into their community
without punishment that was "decisive for the entire person;" it was the fact that he accepted the German officer's
commission in the first instance, as from this all other
future events in his life flowed.

Perhaps we have been overly preoccupied with

"moments" which lead to continued success in the many
stories we have related. But we have also seen that they
can lead to failure. Can there be something in between—
a moment in one's life which can lead to a series of successes and a moment in the same life which can lead as
well to a series of failures? Or a moment which leads to
only one major triumph in one's lifetime as it did for
Herman Melville when he wrote his great American classic, "Moby Dick."

   "I am like one of those seeds taken out of the
Egyptian pyramids which, after being three thousand
years a seed, and nothing but a seed, being planted in
English soil, it developed itself, grew to greeness, and
then fell to the mold. So I," Melville would write his
novelist friend, Nathaniel Hawthorne, in 1851 at the age
of thirty upon the publication of his classic. "Until I was
25, I had no development at all. From my twenty-fifth
year, I date my life. Three weeks scarcely passed at any
time between then and now, that I have not unfolded
myself. But I feel I am now come to the utmost leaf of the
bulb and that shortly the flower must fall to the mold."

   And it did. "Moby Dick" all but consumed
Melville and he produced no other work of such quality
in the next forty years of his life, most of which he spent
as a lowly New York customs inspector, disheartened by
the poor reception accorded his masterpiece. He spent
his final years, debt-ridden and in poor health, seeking
refuge in various forms of mysticism. Vincent Van Gogh

may have felt the same way when he was able to sell only one canvas in his lifetime, and Sigmund Freud when he could not get one word of approval or substantiation for his work from the Medical School or General Hospital where he worked.

One final question remains. If there is a tide in the affairs of men and even nations, and if there is a moment from which all future events flow until they have spent themselves, is it possible to know or anticipate that moment? The answer has to be in the negative. That moment, as we have seen, may come long before the pinnacle of success is reached, in fact be its forerunner; or it may come at the moment of greatest success or even later to mark the beginning of a long series of events leading to eventual decline. Only our good instincts and intuition can suggest to us when that moment has arrived, but we can't be sure. What we do know is that it will pass as nothing unless ambition, courage, determination, hard work, talent, great preparation—and luck—attend it.

> *"There is no one, says another, whom fortune does not visit once in his life; but when she does not find him ready to receive her, she walks in at the door and flies out at the window."*
> Charles de Secondat
> (Baron de Montesquieu)